Great Britain

Inverness &
the Northern
Highlands &
Islands
p887

Stirling &
Central Scotland
p833

⭐Edinburgh p761

Glasgow &
Southern
Scotland
p797

Newcastle &
Northeast England
p617

The Lake District
& Cumbria
p580

Yorkshire
p491

Manchester, Liverpool
& Northwest England
p545

Snowdonia &
North Wales
p722

Birmingham,
the Midlands &
the Marches
p405

Brecon Beacons
& Mid-Wales
p696

Cambridge &
East Anglia
p363

Cardiff, Pembrokeshire
& South Wales
p651

⭐London p66

Bath &
Southwest
England
p232

Canterbury &
Southeast England
p152

Oxford &
the Cotswolds
p187

THIS EDITION WRITTEN AND RESEARCHED BY

Neil Wilson,

Oliver Berry, Fionn Davenport, Marc Di Duca, Belinda Dixon, Peter
Dragicevich, Damian Harper, Catherine Le Nevez, Hugh McNaughtan,
Isabella Noble, Andy Symington

Contents

NATIONAL GALLERY (P80),
LONDON

BIKEWORLDTRAVEL / SHUTTERSTOCK ©

EDINBURGH CASTLE (P763),
SCOTLAND

STEN102 / SHUTTERSTOCK ©

Contents

ON THE ROAD

Contents

Welcome to Great Britain

Buckingham Palace, Stonehenge, Manchester United, The Beatles – Britain does icons like nowhere else, and travel here is a fascinating mix of famous names and hidden gems.

Variety Packed

From the graceful architecture of Canterbury Cathedral to the soaring ramparts of Edinburgh Castle, via the mountains of Wales and the picture-postcard landscape of the Cotswolds, Britain's astounding variety is a major reason to visit. The cities tempt with top-class shops and restaurants, and some of the world's finest museums, while cutting-edge clubs and world-famous theatres provide endless nights to remember. Next day, you're deep in the countryside, high in the hills or enjoying a classic seaside resort. In Britain, there really is something for everyone, whether you're eight or 80, going solo, or travelling with your friends, your kids or your grandma.

Time Travel

A journey through Britain is a journey through history. But not dull and dusty history – this is history you can immerse yourself in. You can lay hands on the megaliths of a 5000-year-old stone circle, or patrol the battlements of a medieval fortress – just as they were patrolled by chain-mail-clad soldiers many centuries ago. Fast-forward to the future and you're admiring 21st-century architecture in Glasgow or exploring the space-age domes of Cornwall's Eden Project.

English Spoken Here

While Britain has a complex culture and esoteric traditions, it feels familiar to many visitors – on the surface, at least – thanks to a vast catalogue of British film and TV exports. And for most visitors, Britain's national language – English – is equally familiar, and one more reason why travel here is a breeze. Of course Wales and Scotland have their own languages, but everyone speaks English too – and all visitors (even Brits) get a little confused by local accents in places such as Devon, Snowdonia and Aberdeen.

Easy Does It

A final thing to remember while you're planning a trip to Britain: getting from place to place is pretty straightforward. Although the locals may grumble (in fact, it's a national pastime), public transport is pretty good and a train ride through the British landscape can be a memorable experience in itself. Whichever way you get around in this compact country, you're never far from the next town, the next pub, the next national park or the next impressive castle on your hit-list of highlights. The choice is endless.

Why I Love Great Britain

By Neil Wilson, Writer

In a word: variety. Few countries pack so much into a small space. Landscapes that range from the sand dunes of South Wales to the snowfields of the Cairngorms, from the lush, quilted farmland of Kent to the naked limestone scarps of the Yorkshire Dales. Three nationalities, two dozen different dialects, more than 60 proudly individual cities, 1000 breweries, 5000 castles – all in a country you could drive across in a day. Plus weather that can offer four seasons in a single afternoon (but remember the old Scandinavian proverb – there's no such thing as bad weather, only the wrong clothes).

For more about our writers, see p1056

Above: Roman Baths (p317), Bath, England

Great Britain

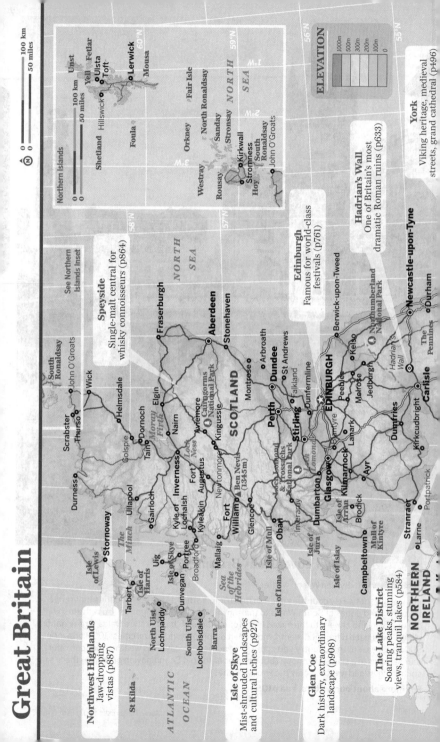

N
0 — 50 miles
0 — 100 km

Northern Islands

0 — 50 miles
0 — 100 km

NORTH SEA

Unst
Yell Fetlar
Uyea
Toft **Lerwick**
Mousa

See Northern
Islands Inset

Shetland Hillswick
Foula

Fair Isle

Speyside
Single-malt central for
whisky connoisseurs (p864)

59°N

Westray
Rousay North Ronaldsay
Kirkwall Sanday
Stromness Stronsay
Hoy South
Ronaldsay
John O'Groats

Orkney

58°N

*NORTH
SEA*

57°N

56°N

55°N

ELEVATION

1000m
500m
300m
200m
100m
0

South
Ronaldsay
John O'Groats
Wick
Scrabster
Thurso

Helmsdale

Northwest Highlands
Jaw-dropping
vistas (p887)

Durness

Golspie
Dornoch
Tain

Fraserburgh **Aberdeen**
Stonehaven

Elgin
Nairn
Moray Firth
Aviemore
Inverness
Kingussie Cairngorms
National Park

Arbroath

Fort
Augustus

Montrose
Dundee
St Andrews

*The
Minch*

Ullapool
Gairloch
Kyle of
Lochalsh
Lochcarron

Newtonmore
Ben Nevis
(1345m)

Perth
Falkland
Dunfermline
Stirling

Berwick-upon-Tweed

Edinburgh
Famous for world-class
festivals (p761)

Isle
of Lewis
Stornoway

St Kilda

*ATLANTIC

OCEAN*

Tarbert
Isle of
Harris

Uig
Isle of Skye
Portree
Dunvegan Broadford
Kyleakin

Mallaig
**Fort
William**
Glencoe

Loch Lomond
& the Trossachs
National Park

Loch
Lomond

Glasgow
Dumbarton Kilmarnock

EDINBURGH
Peebles
Kelso
Melrose
Jedburgh

Northumberland
National Park

*Hadrian's
Wall*

Hadrian's Wall
One of Britain's most
dramatic Roman ruins (p633)

North Uist
Lochmaddy

South Uist
Lochboisdale

Barra

Isle of Skye
Mist-shrouded landscapes
and cultural riches (p927)

Isle of Mull
Oban
Isle of Iona

Isle
of Jura

Inveraray

Brodick
Isle of
Arran

Lanark

Ayr

Dumfries

The
Pennines

Kirkcudbright
Carlisle

Newcastle-upon-Tyne
Durham

Glen Coe
Dark history, extraordinary
landscape (p908)

The Lake District
Soaring peaks, stunning
views, tranquil lakes (p58+)

Isle of Islay

Campbeltown

Mull of
Kintyre

Stranraer
Larne
Portpatrick

**NORTHERN
IRELAND**

York
Viking heritage, medieval
streets, grand cathedral (p496)

SCOTLAND

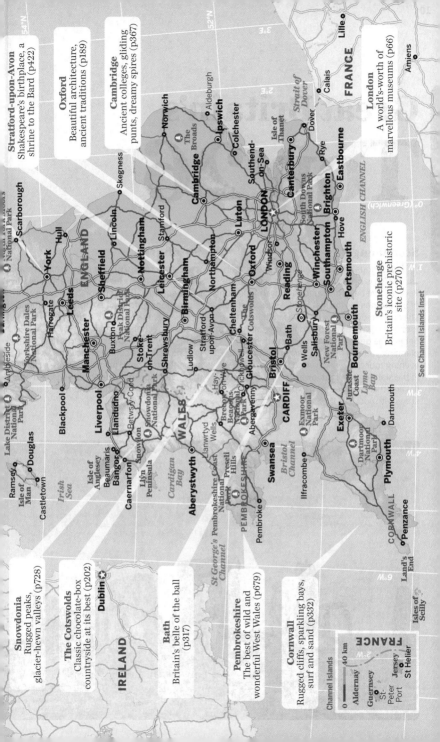

Stratford-upon-Avon
Shakespeare's birthplace, a shrine to the Bard (p422)

Oxford
Beautiful architecture, ancient traditions (p189)

Cambridge
Ancient colleges, gliding punts, dreamy spires (p367)

London
A world's-worth of marvellous museums (p66)

Stonehenge
Britain's iconic prehistoric site (p270)

Snowdonia
Rugged peaks, glacier-hewn valleys (p728)

The Cotswolds
Classic chocolate-box countryside at its best (p202)

Bath
Britain's belle of the ball (p317)

Pembrokeshire
The best of wild and wonderful West Wales (p679)

Cornwall
Rugged cliffs, sparkling bays, surf and sand (p332)

See Channel Islands Inset

Channel Islands
0   40 km

Alderney
Guernsey
St Peter Port
Jersey
St Helier

FRANCE

Great Britain's
Top 26

Stonehenge

1 Mysterious and compelling, Stonehenge (p270) is Britain's most iconic ancient site. People have been drawn to this myth-laden ring of bluestones for the last 5000 years, and we still don't know quite why it was built. Most visitors get to gaze at the 50-tonne megaliths from behind the perimeter fence, but with enough planning you can book an early-morning or evening tour and walk around the inner ring. In the slanting sunlight, away from the crowds, it's an ethereal place – an experience that stays with you.

Edinburgh

2 Edinburgh (p761) is a city of many moods famous for its festivals and especially lively in the summer. It's also worth visiting out of season for sights such as the castle silhouette against a blue spring sky with a yellow haze of daffodils misting the slopes below the esplanade. Or on a chill December morning with the fog snagging the spires of the Old Town, the ancient streets and alleyways more mysterious than ever, rain on the cobblestones and a warm glow beckoning from the window of a pub.

Right: Edinburgh Military Tattoo (p783)

IRISPHOTO1 / SHUTTERSTOCK ©

Bath

3 Britain boasts many great cities, but Bath (p317) stands out as the belle of the ball. Thanks to the natural hot springs that bubble to the surface, the Romans built a health resort here. The waters were rediscovered in the 18th century, and Bath became the place to see and be seen by British high society. Today, the stunning Georgian architecture of grand town houses and sweeping crescents (not to mention Roman remains, a beautiful cathedral and a cutting-edge 21st-century spa) means Bath demands your undivided attention.

Isle of Skye

4 Of all Scotland's many islands, Skye (p927) is one of the most famous and best loved by visitors, thanks to a mix of history (the island's link to Bonnie Prince Charlie is forever remembered by 'The Skye Boat Song'), accessibility (the ferry from the mainland has been replaced by a bridge) and sheer beauty. With jagged mountains, velvet moors and towering sea cliffs, Skye's scenery never fails to impress. And for those days when the mist comes in, there are plenty of castles and local museums to explore, and cosy pubs to enjoy.

The Cotswolds

5 The most wonderful thing about the Cotswolds (p202) is that, no matter where you go or how lost you get, you'll always end up in an impossibly picturesque village complete with rose-clad cottages, an ancient church of honey-coloured stone, a pub with sloping floors and fine ales, and a view of the lush green hills. It's easy to leave the crowds behind and find your very own slice of medieval England – and some of the best boutique hotels in the country.

Above right: Bibury village (p203)

5

Snowdonia

6 The rugged northwest corner of Wales (p728) has rocky mountain peaks, glacier-hewn valleys, sinuous ridges, sparkling lakes and rivers, and charm-infused villages. The busiest part is around Snowdon itself, where many people hike to the summit, and many more take the jolly rack-and-pinion railway, while to the south and west are rarely trod areas perfect for off-the-beaten-track exploration. And just nearby sit the lovely Llŷn Peninsula and Isle of Anglesey, where the sun often shines, even if it's raining on the mountains.

6

SEBASTIEN COELL / SHUTTERSTOCK ©

Oxford

7 For centuries, the brilliant minds and august institutions of Oxford University have made Oxford (p189) famous across the globe. You'll get a glimpse of this revered world as you stroll hushed college quads and cobbled lanes roamed by cycling students and dusty academics. The beautiful college buildings, archaic traditions and stunning architecture have changed little over the centuries, coexisting with a lively, modern, working city.

Football

8 In some parts of the world it's called 'soccer', but here in Britain it's definitely 'football' (p1009). Despite what the fans may say in Italy or Brazil, the English Premier League has some of the world's finest teams. Big names include the globally renowned Arsenal, Liverpool and Chelsea, plus *the* most famous club on the planet: Manchester United. North of the border, Scotland's best-known teams are the Glasgow duo of Rangers and Celtic – their 'old firm' rivalry is legendary – while in Wales the national sport is most definitely rugby.

Bottom: Old Trafford (p555), Manchester

The Lake District

9 William Wordsworth and his Romantic friends were the first to champion the charms of the Lake District (p584), and it's not hard to see what stirred them. The soaring mountains, whaleback fells, razor-edge valleys and – of course – glistening lakes (as well as England's highest peak), make this craggy corner of the country the spiritual home of English hiking. Strap on the boots, stock up on mint cake and drink in the views: inspiration is sure to follow.

Above: Tarn Hows (p595)

Hadrian's Wall

10 Hadrian's Wall (p633) is one of the country's most revealing and dramatic Roman ruins, its 2000-year-old procession of abandoned forts, garrisons, towers and milecastles marching across the wild and lonely landscape of northern England. This wall was about defence and control, but this edge-of-empire barrier also symbolised the boundary of civilised order – to the north lay the unruly land of the marauding Celts, while to the south was the Roman world of orderly taxpaying, underfloor heating and bathrooms.

Castles & Stately Homes

11 Britain's turbulent history is nowhere more apparent than in the mighty castles that dot the landscape, from romantic clifftop ruins such as Corfe (p256) or sturdy fortresses such as Caernarfon, to formidable Stirling and still-inhabited Windsor. And when the aristocracy no longer needed castles, they built vast mansions known as 'stately homes' at the heart of their country estates. Classics of the genre include Blenheim Palace and Chatsworth House in England, Powis Castle in Wales and Scone Palace (pictured) in Scotland.

HELEN HOTSON / SHUTTERSTOCK ©

Cornwall

12 At Britain's far southwestern extremity, the former kingdom of Cornwall (p332) boasts endless miles of coastline with rugged cliffs, sparkling bays, scenic fishing ports and white sandy beaches favoured by everyone from bucket-and-spade families to sun-bronzed surfers. Above the cliffs, the towers of former tin mines now stand like dramatic castles, while inland from the coast is a tranquil landscape of lush farmland and picturesque villages, crowned by the gigantic domes of the Eden Project – a stunning symbol of Cornwall's renaissance.

Above: St Agnes (p362)

Cambridge

13 Abounding with exquisite architecture and steeped in tradition, Cambridge (p367) is a university town extraordinaire. The tightly packed core of ancient colleges, the picturesque riverside 'Backs' (college gardens) and the surrounding green meadows give Cambridge a more tranquil appeal than its historic rival, Oxford. Highlights include the intricate vaulting of King's College Chapel, while no visit is complete without an attempt to steer a punt (flat-bottomed boat) along the river and under the quirky Mathematical Bridge. You'll soon wonder how you could have studied anywhere else.

Stratford-upon-Avon

14 The pretty English Midlands town of Stratford-upon-Avon (p422) is famed around the world as the birthplace of the nation's best-known dramatist, William Shakespeare. Today, the town's tight knot of Tudor streets form a living map of Shakespeare's life and times, while crowds of fans and would-be thespians come to enjoy a play at the theatre or visit the historic houses owned by Shakespeare and his relatives, with a respectful detour to the old stone church where the Bard was laid to rest.

Above: Shakespeare's New Place (p422)

Canterbury Cathedral

15 Few other English cathedrals come close to Canterbury (p156), the top temple of the Anglican Church and a place of worship for over 15 centuries. Its intricate tower dominates the local skyline, its grandeur unsurpassed by later structures. At its heart lies a 12th-century crime scene, the very spot where Archbishop Thomas Becket was put to the sword – an epoch-making event that launched a million pilgrimages and still pulls in the crowds today. A lone candle mourns the gruesome deed, the pink sandstone before it smoothed by 800 years of devout kneeling.

Cardiff

16 The exuberant capital of Wales, compact Cardiff (p653) has emerged as one of Britain's leading urban centres. After a mid-20th-century decline, the city entered the new millennium with vigour and confidence, flexing architectural muscles and revelling in a newfound sense of style. From the historic castle to the ultra-modern waterfront, from lively street cafes to infectious nightlife, from Victorian shopping arcades to the gigantic rugby stadium that is the pulsating heart of the city on match days, Cardiff undoubtedly has buzz.
Bottom: Cardiff Market (p663)

Britain's Pubs

17 Despite the growth of stylish clubs and designer bars, the traditional pub is still the centre of British social life. From the ornate Victorian boozers of London, Edinburgh and Leeds, to the food-focused gastropubs of Yorkshire, Mid-Wales and Devon, and countless rustic country pubs hunkering under thatched roofs and timber beams – Ye Olde Trip to Jerusalem (p456) claims to be the country's oldest – a lunchtime or evening visit to the pub can be one of the best ways to get under the skin of the nation.

Pembrokeshire

18 Perched at the tip of wild and wonderful West Wales, the county of Pembrokeshire (p679) boasts one of Britain's most beautiful and dramatic stretches of coast, with sheer cliffs, natural arches, blowholes, sea stacks, and a wonderful hinterland of tranquil villages and secret waterways. It's a landscape of Norman castles, Iron Age hill forts, holy wells and Celtic saints – including the nation's patron, St David – and intriguing stone monuments left behind by pre-historic inhabitants.

19

HELEN HOTSON / SHUTTERSTOCK ©

20

21

SILVANBACHMANN / SHUTTERSTOCK ©

York

19 With its Roman remains and Viking heritage, ancient city walls and maze of medieval streets, York (p496) is a living showcase for the highlights of English history. Join one of the city's many walking tours and plunge into the network of snickleways (narrow alleys), each the focus of a ghost story or historical character. Explore the intricacies of York Minster (pictured), the biggest medieval cathedral in all of northern Europe, or admire the exhibits from more recent times at the National Railway Museum, the world's largest collection of historic locomotives.

Scotland's Northwest Highlands

20 The Highlands abound in breathtaking views, but the far northwest is truly awe-inspiring. The coastal road between Durness and Kyle of Lochalsh offers jaw-dropping scenes at every turn: the rugged mountains of Assynt (p921), the desolate beauty of Torridon and the remote cliffs of Cape Wrath. Add to this Britain's finest whale-watching, and the nooks of warm Highland hospitality found in classic rural pubs and romantic hotels, make this an unforgettable corner of the country.
Above right: Eilean Donan Castle (p927), Dornie

Liverpool

21 For many visitors, Liverpool (p563) will forever be associated with The Beatles, but a visit here proves the city has much more to offer. After a decade of redevelopment, the waterfront is once again the heart of Liverpool, with Albert Dock declared a World Heritage Site of iconic and protected buildings, a batch of top museums ensuring all sides of the city's history are not forgotten, and the Tate Liverpool gallery and Beatles Story museum, celebrating popular culture and the city's most famous musical sons.

HARRISON EASTWOOD / GETTY IMAGES ©

British Food

22 Britain offers a groaning table full of traditional eating (p982) experiences. Tuck into national favourites such as fish and chips, Cornish pasties or toad in the hole, followed of course by rhubarb and custard or spotted dick, or indulge yourself in a quintessentially English afternoon tea. And don't miss the chance to sample regional specialities such as jellied eels (London), Scottish haggis, Cumberland sausage, Stilton cheese, Northumberland kippers, Lancashire hotpot, Melton Mowbray pork pies, Welsh lamb, Yorkshire pudding... the list goes on.

Above: Pork pie and mustard

Glen Coe

23 Scotland's most famous glen (p908) combines those two essential qualities of the Highland landscape: dramatic scenery and deep history. The peacefulness and beauty of this valley today belie the fact that it was the scene of a ruthless 17th-century massacre, when the local MacDonalds were murdered by soldiers of the Campbell clan. Some of the glen's finest walks – to the Lost Valley, for example – follow the routes used by the clanspeople trying to flee their attackers, and where many perished in the snow.

Above right: Red deer, Rannoch Moor (p907)

Whisky

24 After tea, Britain's best-known drink is whisky. And while this amber spirit is also made in England and Wales, it is always most associated with Scotland. With more than 2000 whisky brands available, there are distilleries dotted all over Scotland, many open to visitors, with Speyside (p864) one of the main concentrations and a favourite spot for connoisseurs. Before enjoying your tipple, heed these warnings: never spell whisky with an 'e' (that's the Irish variety); and when ordering at the bar, never ask for 'Scotch'. What else would you drink in Scotland?

Money

ATMs (usually called 'cash machines') are common in cities and towns, but watch out for tampering; a common ruse is to attach a cardreader to the slot. Visa and MasterCard are widely accepted in Britain, except at some smaller B&Bs which take cash or cheque only. Other credit cards, including Amex, are not so widely accepted. Cities and larger towns have banks and exchange bureaux for changing money into pounds, but some bureaux offer poor rates. You can change money at some post offices, which is very handy in country areas; exchange rates are fair.

Bargaining

A bit of mild haggling is acceptable at flea markets and antique shops, but everywhere else you're expected to pay the advertised price.

Tipping

Restaurants Around 10% in restaurants and teashops with table service. Nearer 15% at smarter restaurants. Tips may be added to your bill as a 'service charge'. Paying a tip or a service charge is not obligatory.

Pubs & Bars Not expected unless table service for your meal and drinks is provided, then 10% is usual.

Taxis Around 10%, or rounded up to the nearest pound, especially in London.

MARCO PRATI / SHUTTERSTOCK ©

Antiques stall, Apple Market, Covent Garden (p81)

Etiquette

Manners The British have a reputation for being polite, and good manners are considered important in most situations. When asking directions, 'Excuse me, can you tell me the way to...' is a better tactic than 'Hey, where's...'

Queues In Britain, queueing ('standing in line' to Americans), whether to board a bus, buy tickets or enter the gates of an attraction, is sacrosanct. Any attempt to 'jump the queue' will result in an outburst of tutting and hard stares.

Escalators If you take an escalator or a moving walkway (especially at tube stations in London), be sure to stand on the right, so folks in a hurry can pass on the left.

Eating

It's wise to book ahead for midrange restaurants, especially at weekends. Top-end restaurants should be booked at least a couple of weeks in advance.

Restaurants Britain's restaurants range from cheap-and-cheerful to Michelin-starred, and cover every cuisine you can imagine.

Cafes Open during daytime (rarely after 6pm), cafes are good for a casual breakfast or lunch, or simply a cup of coffee.

Pubs Most of Britain's pubs serve reasonably priced meals, and many can compete with restaurants on quality.

What's New

The Night Tube

It only took 153 years since its opening day, but London's Underground railway has finally begun operating around the clock (on Friday and Saturday nights). (p151)

Shakespeare's School Room

The Stratford school room where the world's most famous playwright was taught the three Rs from 1571 to 1578 was opened to the public in 2016. (p423)

Lakes Distillery

Watch out, Scotland! The first English whisky distillery for more than a century has opened in Keswick; its first single malt will be available from 2018. (p605)

i360 Tower

Sprouting from the ashes of Brighton's historic West Pier (destroyed by fire in 2003), this futuristic 162m-tall tower with circular glass viewing pod is Brighton's answer to the London Eye. (p179)

Magna Carta

The 800th anniversary of the signing of the Magna Carta in 2015 saw a £22m restoration of Lincoln Castle create a subterranean vault to house one of only four original copies of this iconic document. (p460)

Zip World Blaenau Ffestiniog

Blaenau Ffestiniog's vast Llechwedd Slate Caverns now have the added thrill of zip lines, trampolines, walkways and nets suspended over cathedral-sized voids. (p733)

York City Art Gallery

Yorkshire's reputation as the epicentre of UK sculpture was further enhanced with the opening in 2015 of the revamped York Art Gallery's Centre of Ceramic Arts. (p501)

Sky Garden

One of London's recent landmark skyscrapers, 20 Fenchurch St (nicknamed the Walkie Talkie), now has free access to its spectacular 155m-high rooftop garden and viewing gallery. (p135)

V&A Museum of Design

Dundee's waterfront is graced by a stunning new building that is home to an outpost of London's Victoria & Albert Museum, a showcase for the best of Scottish art and design. (p852)

North Coast 500

This 500-mile circuit (www.northcoast 500.com) of northern Scotland's stunning coastline has proved an overnight hit, with thousands of people completing the route by car, campervan, motorbike or bicycle. (p923)

Borders Railway

The longest stretch of new railway line to be built in the UK for more than 100 years opened in September 2015, linking Edinburgh with Tweedbank, near Melrose (www.bordersrailway.co.uk).

For more recommendations and reviews, see lonelyplanet.com/great-britain

If You Like...

Castles & Stately Homes

Tower of London (p83) Landmark of the capital, patrolled by famous Beefeaters and protected by legendary ravens.

Blenheim Palace (p201) A monumental baroque fantasy and one of Britain's greatest stately homes.

Castle Howard (p506) A stunning baroque edifice, best known as the setting for TV series *Brideshead Revisited*.

Warwick Castle (p419) Restored enough to be impressive, ruined enough to be romantic.

Stirling Castle (p836) Classic fortress atop volcanic crag, with stunning views from the battlements.

Beaumaris Castle (p754) Wales is the land of castles; imposing Beaumaris, along with nearby Conwy, Caernarfon and Harlech, is a jointly listed World Heritage Site.

Chatsworth House (p489) The quintessential stately home, a treasure trove of heirlooms and works of art.

Carreg Cennen (p706) The most dramatically positioned fortress in Wales, standing guard over a lonely stretch of Brecon Beacons National Park.

Cathedrals & Ruined Abbeys

St Paul's Cathedral (p85) A symbol of the city for centuries, and still an essential part of the London skyline.

York Minster (p496) One of the largest medieval cathedrals in all of Europe, especially renowned for its windows.

Fountains Abbey (p514) Extensive ruins set in more recently landscaped water gardens – one of the most beautiful sites in Britain.

Canterbury Cathedral (p156) The mother ship of the Anglican Church, still attracting pilgrims and visitors in their thousands.

Melrose Abbey (p822) The finest of all the great Border abbeys; Robert the Bruce's heart is buried here.

Whitby Abbey (p518) Stunning clifftop ruin with an eerie atmosphere that inspired the author of *Dracula*.

St David's Cathedral (p686) An ancient place of worship in Britain's smallest city.

Glastonbury Abbey (p330) The legendary burial place of King Arthur and Queen Guinevere.

Glasgow Cathedral (p801) A shining example of Gothic architecture, and the only mainland Scottish cathedral to have survived the Reformation.

Tintern Abbey (p666) Riverside ruins that inspired generations of poets and artists.

Royal Britain

Buckingham Palace (p73) The Queen's official London residence, best known for its royal-waving balcony and the Changing of the Guard.

Windsor Castle (p225) The largest and oldest occupied fortress in the world, a majestic vision of battlements and towers, and the Queen's weekend retreat.

Westminster Abbey (p70) Where English royalty is crowned and married – most recently William and Kate.

Royal Yacht Britannia (p778) The royal family's onetime floating home during foreign travels, now retired and moored near Edinburgh.

Balmoral Castle (p903) Built for Queen Victoria in 1855 and still a royal Highland hideaway.

Royal Pavilion (p177) Opulent palace built for playboy prince, later King George IV.

Althorp House (p467) Ancestral home and burial place of Diana, Princess of Wales.

Village Idylls

Lavenham (p386) A wonderful collection of exquisitely preserved medieval buildings virtually untouched since the 15th century.

Lacock (p273) Well-preserved medieval village, essentially free of modern development and – unsurprisingly – a frequent set for movies and TV period dramas.

Culross (p851) Scotland's best-preserved 17th-century village, familiar to fans of TV's *Outlander* as Cranesmuir.

Goathland (p523) One of Yorkshire's most attractive villages, complete with village green and traditional steam railway station.

Mousehole (p347) Southwest England overflows with picturesque pint-sized ports, but this is one of the best.

Beddgelert (p738) A conservation village of rough grey stone buildings in the heart of Snowdonia National Park.

Great Outdoors

Lake District (p584) The landscape that inspired William Wordsworth is a feast of mountains, valleys, views and – of course – lakes.

Northumberland National Park (p640) The dramatically empty landscape of England's far north is remote and off the beaten track.

Snowdonia (p728) The best-known slice of nature in Wales, with the grand but surprisingly accessible peak of Snowdon at its heart.

Top: Culross (p851)
Bottom: Kelvingrove Art Gallery & Museum (p805), Glasgow

Britain's Footpath Network

Britain is covered in a vast network of footpaths, many of which are centuries old, dating from the time when walking was the only way to get from farm to village, from village to town, from town to coast, or from valley to valley. Any walk you do today will follow these historic paths. Even Britain's longest walks simply link up many shorter paths. You'll also sometimes walk along 'bridleways', originally used for horse transport, and old unsurfaced roads called 'byways'.

Rights of Way

The absolute pleasure of walking in Britain is mostly thanks to the 'right of way' network – public paths and tracks across private property, especially in England and Wales. In Britain, nearly all land (including in national parks) is privately owned, but if there's a right of way you can follow it through fields, pastures, woods, even farmhouse yards, as long as you keep to the route and do no damage. In some mountain and moorland areas, walkers can move freely beyond the rights of way and explore at will. Known as 'freedom to roam', where permitted it's clearly advertised with markers on gates and signposts. For more information see the Access pages on www.naturalengland.org.uk.

Scotland has a different legal system, where the Scottish Outdoor Access Code (www.outdooraccess-scotland.com) allows walkers to cross most private land providing they act responsibly. There are restrictions during lambing time, bird-nesting periods and the grouse- and deer-hunting seasons.

Britain's Best Walking Areas

Although you can walk just about anywhere in Britain, some areas are better than others. Here's a rundown of favourite places, suitable for short walks of a couple of hours, or longer all-day outings.

Southern England

The chalky hills of the South Downs stride across the counties of West Sussex and East Sussex, while the New Forest in Hampshire is great for easy strolls and the nearby Isle of Wight has excellent walking options. The highest and wildest area in southern England is Dartmoor, dotted

WEATHER WATCH

While enjoying the outdoors, it's always worth remembering the fickle nature of the British weather. The countryside can appear gentle and welcoming, and often is, but sometimes conditions can turn nasty – especially on the higher ground. At any time of year, if you're walking on the hills or open moors, it's vital to be well equipped. You should carry warm and waterproof clothing (even in summer); a map and compass (that you know how to use); and drink and food, including high-energy stuff such as chocolate. If you're really going off the beaten track, leave details of your route with someone.

with Bronze Age remains and granite outcrops called 'tors' – looking for all the world like abstract sculptures. Exmoor has heather-covered hills cut by deep valleys and a lovely stretch of coastline, while the entire coast of the southwest peninsula from Dorset to Somerset offers dramatic walking conditions – especially along the beautiful cliff-lined shore of Cornwall.

Central England

The gem of central England is the Cotswolds, classic English countryside with gentle paths through neat fields, mature woodland and pretty villages of honey-coloured stone. The Marches, where England borders Wales, are similarly bucolic with more good walking options. For something higher, aim for the Peak District, divided into two distinct areas: the White Peak, characterised by limestone, farmland and verdant dales, ideal for gentle strolls; and the Dark Peak, with high peaty moorlands, heather and gritstone outcrops, for more serious hikes.

Northern England

The Lake District is the heart and soul of walking in England, a wonderful area of soaring peaks, endless views, deep valleys and, of course, beautiful lakes. On the other side of the country, the rolling hills of the Yorkshire Dales make it another very popular walking area. Further north, keen walkers love the starkly beautiful hills of

LONG-DISTANCE TRAILS

Some long-distance walking routes – such as the Pennine Way, the West Highland Way and the Pembrokeshire Coast Path – are well known and well maintained, with signposts and route-markers along the way, as well as being highlighted on Ordnance Survey maps. The most high-profile of these are the national trails, usually very clearly marked on the ground and on the map – ideal for beginners or visitors from overseas (although they're easy to follow, it doesn't mean they're necessarily easy underfoot). A downside of these famous routes is that they can be crowded in holiday times, making accommodation harder to find. An upside is the great feeling of camaraderie with other walkers on the trail.

Northumberland National Park, while the nearby coast is less daunting but just as dramatic – perfect for wild seaside strolls.

South & Mid-Wales

The Brecon Beacons is a large range of gigantic rolling whaleback hills with broad ridges and table-top summits, while out in the west is Pembrokeshire, a wonderful array of beaches, cliffs, islands, coves and harbours, with a hinterland of tranquil farmland and secret waterways, and a relatively mild climate year-round.

North Wales

For walkers, North Wales *is* Snowdonia, where the remains of ancient volcanoes bequeath a striking landscape of jagged peaks, ridges and cliffs. There are challenging walks on Snowdon itself – at 1085m, the highest peak in Wales – and many more on the nearby Glyderau and Carneddau ranges, or further south around Cader Idris.

Southern & Central Scotland

This extensive region embraces several areas just perfect for keen walkers, including Ben Lomond, the best-known peak in the area, and the nearby hills of the Trossachs, lying within the Loch Lomond and The Trossachs National Park. Also

here is the splendid Isle of Arran, with a great choice of coastal rambles and high-mountain hikes.

Northern & Western Scotland

For serious walkers, heaven is the northern and western parts of Scotland, where the forces of nature have created a mountainous landscape of utter grandeur, including two of Scotland's most famous place names, Glen Coe and Ben Nevis (Britain's highest mountain at 1345m). Off the west coast lie the dramatic mountains of the Isle of Skye. Keep going north along the western coast, and things just keep getting better: a remote and beautiful area, sparsely populated, with scenic glens and lochs, and some of the largest, wildest and finest mountains in Britain.

Cycling & Mountain Biking

A bike is the perfect mode of transport for exploring back-road Britain. Once you escape the busy main highways, a vast network of quiet country lanes winds through fields and peaceful villages, ideal for cycletouring. You can cruise through gently rolling landscapes, taking it easy and stopping for cream teas, or you can thrash all day through hilly areas, revelling in steep ascents and swooping downhill sections. You can cycle from place to place, camping or staying in B&Bs (many of which are cyclist-friendly), or you can base yourself in one area for a few days and go out on rides in different directions. All you need is a map and a sense of adventure.

Mountain-bikers can go further into the wilds on the tracks and bridleways that criss-cross Britain's hills and high moors, or head for the many dedicated mountainbike trail centres where specially built single-track winds through the forests. Options at these centres vary from delightful dirt roads ideal for families to gnarly rock gardens and precipitous dropoffs for hardcore riders, all classified from green to black in ski-resort style.

www.sustrans.org.uk Details of Britain's national network of cycling trails.

www.forestry.gov.uk/england-cycling Guide to forest cycling trails in England.

www.dmbins.com Guide to mountain-biking trails in Scotland.

Fishing

After walking, fishing is Britain's most popular outdoor activity. As well as sea angling, there is excellent fishing for brown trout, grayling, pike, perch, carp and other coarse fish all over the country, while Scotland offers some of the world's best salmon fishing.

Fishing rights to most inland waters are privately owned and you must obtain a permit to fish in them – these are usually readily available from the local fishing-tackle shop or hotel, which are also great sources of advice and local knowledge. Permits cost from around £5 to £20 per day, but salmon fishing on some rivers – notably the Tyne in northeast England, and Scotland's Tweed, Tay and Spey – can be much more expensive (up to £150 a day).

In England and Wales, as well as a permit you will need a rod licence, which can be purchased online (www.postoffice.co.uk/rod-fishing-licence) or from post offices all over the country. This costs £3.75/10/27 for one day/eight days/one year for all freshwater fish except salmon and sea trout, which cost £8/23/72. Rod licences are not required in Scotland.

Fishing in the sea is generally free (except for salmon and sea trout), and neither permit nor rod licence is needed.

www.fishpal.com Information and booking portal for fishing (mostly salmon and trout) all over Britain.

www.fishing.visitwales.com Guide to fishing in Wales.

Surfing & Windsurfing

Britain may not seem an obvious destination for surfing, but conditions are surprisingly good and the large tidal range often means a completely different set of breaks at low and high tides. If you've come from the other side of the world, you'll be delighted to learn that summer water temperatures in southern England are roughly equivalent to winter temperatures in southern Australia (ie you'll still need a wetsuit). At the main spots, it's easy enough to hire boards and wetsuits.

Top of the list are the Atlantic-facing coasts of Cornwall and Devon (Newquay is surf-central, with all the trappings from Kombi vans to bleached hair), and there are smaller surf scenes elsewhere, notably Pembrokeshire and the Gower in Wales, and Norfolk and Yorkshire in eastern England. Hardier souls can head for northern Scotland and the Outer Hebrides, which have some of the best and most consistent surf in Europe.

Windsurfing is hugely popular all around the coast. Top areas include Norfolk, Suffolk, Devon and Cornwall, the Isle of Wight, and the islands of Tiree, Orkney and the Outer Hebrides.

www.surfinggb.com Listings of approved surf schools, courses, competitions and so on.

www.ukwindsurfing.com A good source of info.

Canoeing, Kayaking & Rafting

Britain's west coast, with its sheltered inlets, indented shoreline and countless islands, is ideal for sea kayaking, while its inland lakes and canals are great for Canadian canoeing. In addition, the turbulent spate rivers of Scotland and Wales offers some of Britain's best whitewater kayaking and rafting.

Equipment rental and instruction are readily available in major centres such as Cornwall, Anglesey, the Lake District, Loch Lomond and the Isle of Skye.

www.gocanoeing.org.uk Lists approved canoeing centres in England.

www.canoescotland.org Canoe trails in Scotland.

www.ukrafting.co.uk Whitewater rafting in Wales.

Coasteering

If sometimes a simple clifftop walk just won't cut the mustard, then coasteering might appeal. It's like mountaineering, but instead of going up a mountain, you go sideways along a coast – a steep and rocky coast – with waves breaking around your feet. And if the rock gets too steep, no problem – you jump in and start swimming. Coasteering centres provide wetsuits, helmets and buoyancy aids; you provide an old pair of training shoes and a sense of adventure. The sport is available all around Britain, but the mix of sheer cliffs, sandy beaches and warmer water make Cornwall and Devon prime spots.

www.coasteering.org Info on coasteering in Devon and Cornwall.

Rock Climbing

Britain has a long history of rock climbing and mountaineering, with many of the classic routes having been pioneered in the 19th century. The main rock-climbing areas include the Scottish Highlands, the Lake District, the Peak District and North Wales, plus the sea cliffs of South Wales, Devon and Cornwall, but there are also hundreds of smaller crags situated all over the country.

Comprehensive climbing guidebooks are published by the Scottish Mountaineering Club (www.smc.org.uk), the Fell & Rock Climbing Club (www.frcc.co.uk) and the Climbers Club (www.climbersclub.co.uk).

www.ukclimbing.com Full of useful information.

Horse Riding & Pony Trekking

If you want to explore the hills and moors but walking or cycling is too much of a sweat, seeing the wilder parts of Britain from horseback is highly recommended. In rural areas and national parks like Dartmoor and Northumberland, riding centres cater to all levels of proficiency, with ponies for kids and beginners and horses for the more experienced.

British Horse Society (www.bhs.org.uk) Lists approved riding centres offering day rides or longer holidays on horseback.

Sailing & Boating

Scotland's west coast, with its myriad islands, superb scenery and challenging winds and tides, is widely acknowledged to be one of the finest yachting areas in the world, while the canals of England and Wales offer a classic narrow-boating experience.

Beginners can take a Royal Yachting Association (www.rya.org.uk) training course in yachting or dinghy sailing at many sailing schools around the coast. Narrow-boaters only need a quick introductory lesson at the start of their trip – for more info see www.canal holidays.com.

Skiing & Snowboarding

Britain's ski centres are all in the Scottish Highlands:

Cairngorm Mountain (www.cairngormmountain. org) 1097m; has almost 30 runs spread over an extensive area.

Glencoe (www.glencoemountain.com) 1108m; has five tows and two chairlifts.

Glenshee (www.ski-glenshee.co.uk) 920m; situated on the A93 road between Perth and Braemar; offers the largest network of lifts and the widest range of runs in Britain.

Lecht (www.lecht.co.uk) 793m; the smallest and most remote centre, on the A939 between Ballater and Grantown-on-Spey.

Nevis Range (www.nevisrange.co.uk) 1221m; near Fort William; offers the highest ski runs, the grandest setting and some of the best off-piste potential.

The high season is from January to April, but it's sometimes possible to ski from as early as November to as late as May. It's easy to turn up at the slopes, hire some kit, buy a day pass and off you go.

Weather and snow reports can be obtained from:

Ski Scotland (www.ski-scotland.com)

WinterHighland (www.winterhighland.info)

Lancashire hotpot (p49)

Plan Your Trip
Eat & Drink Like a Local

Britain once had a reputation for bad food, but the nation has enjoyed something of a culinary revolution over the past decade and a half. London is recognised as having one of the best restaurant scenes in the world, while all over the country stylish eateries and gourmet gastropubs are making the most of a newfound passion for quality local produce.

The Year in Food

Best in Spring (Mar–May)

Spring brings fresh asparagus, new potatoes (notably Jersey Royals), pink rhubarb and tender lamb.

Best in Summer (Jun–Aug)

Strawberries, raspberries and other soft fruits are in season along with salad vegetables such as lettuce and radishes, and seafood such as scallops, langoustines, mackerel and cod.

Best in Autumn (Sep–Nov)

Apples and blackberries (often cooked together in a crumble), game including venison and wood pigeon, and shellfish – oysters, mussels and cockles. Also the main season for food festivals.

Best in Winter (Dec–Feb)

Sweet chestnuts (roasted on an open fire), and that classic Christmas combination of goose, root vegetables and Brussels sprouts.

Food Experiences

Meals of a Lifetime

Waterside Inn (p229) Exquisite French food at Alain Roux's classic restaurant, in a romantic setting on the banks of the Thames.

Dinner by Heston Blumenthal (p128) Famous exponent of 'molecular gastronomy' leads you through a tour of Britain's culinary history.

Restaurant Nathan Outlaw (p337) Superb local seafood is the trademark of Cornwall's only Michelin-starred chef.

Three Chimneys (p933) A windswept crofting cottage in a far-flung corner of the Isle of Skye is home to unexpected gastronomic delights.

Hardwick (p667) Set in the heart of mid-Wales gastropub territory, this rustic inn was one of the first on the scene, and still delivers a meal to remember.

St John (p133) A pioneer of 'nose-to-tail' dining (ie eating every part of the animal), St John offers a memorably 'offal' dining experience.

Cheap Treats

Bacon sandwich The breakfast of champions. Debate rages over the choice of sauce – red (tomato ketchup) or brown (spicy pickled fruit sauce).

Beans on toast A comforting childhood classic of tinned baked beans poured over buttered toast, served in many cafes as a breakfast or lunch dish.

Fish and chips The nation's favourite takeaway meal, served in hundreds of chip shops all over the country.

Cockles A classic seaside snack that has been enjoyed by generations of British holidaymakers, sprinkled with vinegar and eaten from a cardboard tub with a wooden fork.

Scotch egg This masterpiece of culinary engineering consists of a hardboiled egg wrapped in sausage meat, coated in breadcrumbs and deep-fried.

Dare to Try

Haggis Scotland's national dish is made from the chopped heart, liver and lungs of a sheep, mixed with oatmeal and onion. Widely available in Scottish restaurants.

Tripe Cow's stomach lining, traditionally poached in milk with onions. A wartime staple, but hard to find in restaurants today – though it's making a comeback.

Stinking Bishop Britain's most pungent cheese, made in Gloucestershire and redolent of old socks. Available from Harrods in London, and many specialist cheese shops.

Jellied eels Traditional London side dish that can still be found in the capital's pie and mash shops.

Local Specialities

Scotland

Scotland may be most famous for haggis, but seafood is where it excels. Fresh lobster, langoustine, salmon and scallops are the favourites of restaurant menus, but look out for traditional dishes such as Arbroath smokies (hot-smoked haddock) and Cullen skink (soup made with smoked haddock, onion, butter and milk). Oats have been a mainstay of the Scottish diet for centuries, appearing in the form of porridge and oatcakes, but also as a coating for fried trout or herring, and in the classic Scottish dessert known as cranachan (whipped cream flavoured with whisky and mixed with raspberries and toasted oatmeal).

Wales

Tender and tasty Welsh lamb is sought after by restaurateurs all over Britain, but it also appears in the rustic local dish known as cawl (pronounced cowl) – a one-pot stew of lamb, bacon, cabbage, potato and swede. Better known is laverbread, which is not bread but seaweed, cooked with oatmeal and often served for breakfast with toast and bacon. Sweet-toothed visitors should look out for Welsh cakes (fruity griddle scones) and bara brith (a dense and spicy fruit cake flavoured with tea and marmalade).

The English Midlands

The Leicestershire town of Melton Mowbray is famed for its pork pies, always eaten cold, ideally with pickle. Only pies handmade in the eponymous town can carry the Melton Mowbray moniker – in the same way that only fizzy wine from the Champagne region of France can carry that name.

Another British speciality from this region that enjoys the same protection is Stilton – a strong white cheese, either plain or blue vein. Only five dairies in all of Britain (four of which are in Derbyshire) are allowed to name the cheese they produce Stilton. Bizarrely, the cheese cannot be made in the village of Stilton in Cambridgeshire, although this is where it was first sold – hence the name.

North of England

The northeast of England is known for its kippers (smoked herring), traditionally grilled with butter and served for breakfast with toast and marmalade on the side, and for pease pudding (a thick stew of yellow split peas cooked in ham stock). The northwest lays claim to Lancashire hotpot (slow-cooked stew of lamb and onion topped with sliced potatoes), Eccles cakes (rounds of flaky pastry filled with currants), and Cumberland sausage (a spiral shaped pork sausage flavoured with herbs). But the most famous of northern specialities is Yorkshire pudding, a light and puffy

Fish and chips

batter pudding usually served as a side dish with roast beef, that has now been adopted all over Britain.

Southwest England

Cows reared on the rich pastures of Devon and Cornwall create some of Britain's finest dairy produce, notably the famous clotted cream (a very thick cream made by heating full-cream milk) that forms an essential component of Cornish cream teas. Less refined but equally tasty are Cornish pasties (crimped pastry parcels containing cooked vegetables and, less traditionally, minced beef), once the lunchtime staple of miners and farm workers.

London & Southeast England

Ask a Londoner about local food specialities, and you're bound to get the answer: pie and mash, and jellied eels. The staple menu of working-class Londoners since the 19th century, the former consists of a small pie filled with minced beef served with mashed potato and 'liquor' – a parsley-rich gravy made from the stock in which eels have been cooked. The eels are cooled and

Dinner by Heston Blumenthal (p128), London

set in the jellied stock, and served as a side dish with malt vinegar – try them out at M Manze or Poppies.

Oysters today have an expensive reputation, but in the 19th century they were a cheap and plentiful foodstuff, eaten by all. Whitstable oysters, from Kent – the native British species, unlike the more common, farmed Pacific oysters – have been harvested since Roman times, and still grace the tables of London restaurants and oyster bars.

How to Eat & Drink

In parts of Britain, notably northern England and Scotland, many people use the word 'dinner' for their main midday meal, and 'tea' for a light evening meal. However, this terminology is rarely, if ever, used in restaurants.

When to Eat

Breakfast Served in most hotels and B&Bs between 7am and 9am, or perhaps 8am to 10am on weekends. In cafes, the breakfast menu might extend to 11am through the week. For many visitors, the first meal of the day is what's known as the 'Full English Breakfast' – aka Full Welsh, Scottish, Yorkshire etc – a plateful of fried food that might shock if you're expecting just a bowl of cereal. But it can fuel several hours of energetic sightseeing.

Lunch Generally taken between noon and 2pm, and can range from a sandwich and a bag of crisps to a three-course meal with wine. Many restaurants offer a set menu two-course lunch at competitive prices on weekdays, while cafes often have a daily lunch special, or offer soup and a sandwich.

Afternoon tea A tradition inherited from the British aristocracy and eagerly adopted by the middle classes, a between-meals snack now enjoying a revival in country hotels and upmarket tearooms. It consists of dainty sandwiches, cakes and pastries, plus, of course, a cup of tea, poured from a silver teapot and sipped politely from fine china cups.

Dinner The main meal of the day, usually served in restaurants between 6pm and 9pm, and

Afternoon tea

GREAT BRITISH CHEESES

Cheddar Sharp and savoury, Britain's most popular cheese originates in Somerset but is now made all over the country (and, indeed, the world).

Stilton A pungent blue cheese, traditionally eaten after dinner with a glass of port.

Wensleydale Crumbly white cheese from Yorkshire, with a mild, honeyed flavour.

Caerphilly From the Welsh town of the same name, this hard, salty cheese has an annual festival dedicated to it.

Cornish Yarg A rich, creamy cheese characterised by its wrapping of nettle leaves.

Caboc A Highland Scottish cream cheese rolled in oatmeal, whose recipe is more than 500 years old.

consisting of two or three courses – starter, main and dessert. Upmarket restaurants might serve a five-course dinner, with an amuse-bouche to begin, and a fish course between starter and main.

Sunday lunch Another great British tradition. It is the main meal of the day, normally served between noon and 4pm. Many pubs and restaurants offer Sunday lunch, where the main course usually consists of roast beef, lamb or pork, accompanied by roast and mashed potatoes, gravy, and boiled vegetables such as carrots and peas.

Where to Eat

Cafes Traditional cafes are simple eateries serving simple food – sandwiches, pies, sausage and chips. Quality varies enormously: some cafes definitely earn their 'greasy spoon' handle, while others are neat and clean.

Tearooms The tearoom is a British institution, serving cakes, scones and sandwiches accompanied by pots of tea (though coffee is usually available too). Upmarket tearooms may also serve afternoon tea.

Coffee shops In most cities and towns you'll also find coffee shops – both independents and international chains – serving decent lattes, cappuccinos and espressos, and continental-style snacks such as bagels, panini and ciabattas.

Restaurants London has scores of excellent restaurants that could hold their own in major cities worldwide, while eating places in other British cities can give the capital a run for its money (often for rather less money).

Pubs Many British pubs serve a wide range of food, and it's often a good-value option whether you want a toasted sandwich between museum visits in London, or a three-course meal in the evening after touring the castles of Wales.

Gastropubs The quality of food in some pubs is now so high that they have created a whole new genre of eatery – the gastropub. The finest are almost restaurants (a few have been awarded Michelin stars), but others go for a more relaxed atmosphere.

Plan Your Trip
Travel with Children

Britain is ideal for travelling with children because of its compact size, packing a lot of attractions into a small area. So when the kids in the back of the car ask 'Are we there yet?', your answer can often be 'Yes, we are'.

Best Regions for Kids

London
The capital has children's attractions galore; many are free.

Southwest England
Lovely beaches and reliable weather, though crowded in summer.

The Midlands
Caverns and 'show caves', plus former railways now traffic-free cycle routes.

Oxford & the Cotswolds
Oxford has Harry Potter connections; the Cotswolds is ideal for little-leg strolls.

Lake District & Cumbria
Zip wires and kayaks for teenagers; boat rides and Beatrix Potter for youngsters.

Wales
Long coast of beaches and pony-trekking in the hill country. And loads of castles...

Southern Scotland
Edinburgh and Glasgow have kid-friendly museums; the Southern Uplands offer great mountain biking for a range of skill levels.

Scottish Highlands & Islands
Hardy teenagers plunge into outdoor activities; dolphin-spotting boat trips are fun for all the family.

Great Britain for Kids

Many places of interest cater for kids as much as adults. At historic castles, for example, mum and dad can admire the medieval architecture, while the kids will have great fun striding around the battlements. In the same way, many national parks and holiday resorts organise specific activities for children. It goes without saying that everything ramps up in the school holidays.

Bargain Hunting

Most visitor attractions offer family tickets – usually two adults plus two children – for less than the sum of the individual entrance charges. Most offer cheaper rates for solo parents and kids, too. Be sure to ask, as these are not always clearly displayed.

On the Road

If you're going by public transport, trains are great for families: intercity services have plenty of room for luggage and extra stuff like buggies (strollers), and the kids can move about a bit when bored. In contrast, they need to stay in their seats on long-distance coaches.

If you're hiring a car, most (but not all) rental firms can provide child seats – but you'll need to check this in advance. Most will not actually fit the child seats; you need to do that yourself, for insurance reasons.

Dining, not Whining

When it comes to refuelling, most cafes and teashops are child-friendly. Restaurants are mixed: some offer high chairs and kiddy portions; others firmly say 'no children after 6pm'.

Children under 18 are usually not allowed in pubs serving just alcohol. Pubs also serving meals generally allow children of any age (with their parents) in England and Wales, but in Scotland they must be over 14 and must leave by 8pm. If in doubt, simply ask the bar staff.

And finally, a word on another kind of refuelling: Britain is still slightly buttoned up about breastfeeding. Older folks may tut-tut a bit if you give junior a top-up in public, but if done modestly it's usually considered OK.

Children's Highlights

Best Fresh-Air Fun

If the kids tire of castles and museums, you're never far from a place for outdoor activities to blow away the cobwebs.

Wildlife Cruises, Scotland's west coast (p872) What child could resist a boat trip to see seals, porpoises and dolphins, maybe even a whale?

Puzzlewood, Forest of Dean (p220) Wonderful woodland playground with mazy paths, weird rock formations and eerie passageways.

Whinlatter Forest Park, Cumbria (p605) Highlights include a Go Ape adventure park and excellent mountain-bike trails, plus live video feeds from red-squirrel cams.

Bewilderwood, Norfolk (p400) Zip wires, jungle bridges, tree houses, marsh walks, boat trips, mazes and all sorts of old-fashioned outdoor adventure.

Lyme Regis, Dorset (p264) Guided tours to find your very own prehistoric fossil.

Cotswold Farm Park (p210) Child-friendly introduction to the world of farm animals.

Tissington Trail, Derbyshire (p479) Cycling this former railway is fun and almost effortless. You can hire kids' bikes, tandems and trailers. Don't forget to hoot in the tunnels!

7Stanes MTB Centres, Southern Scotland (p829) A network of mountain-biking centres offering everything from easy, family-friendly trails with picnic tables and viewpoints, to more challenging routes for teenagers.

Best Hands-On Action

Please do not touch? No chance. Here are some places where grubby fingers and enquiring minds are positively welcomed.

Science Museum, London (p94) Seven floors of educational exhibits, at the mother of all science museums.

Enginuity, Ironbridge (p443) Endless hands-on displays at the birthplace of the Industrial Revolution.

National Waterfront Museum, Swansea (p671) Great interactive family fun.

Glasgow Science Centre (p805) Bringing science and technology alive through hundreds of engaging exhibits.

Discovery Museum, Newcastle (p621) Tyneside's rich history on display; highlights include a buzzers-and-bells science maze.

At-Bristol, Bristol (p311) One of Britain's best interactive science museums, covering space, technology and the human brain.

Riverside Museum, Glasgow (p804) Top-class interactive museum with a focus on transport.

Jorvik Viking Centre, York (p499) Excellent smells-and-all Viking settlement reconstruction.

Natural History Museum, London (p94) Highlights include the life-size blue whale and animatronic dinosaurs.

BABY-CHANGING FACILITIES

Most museums and other attractions in Britain usually have good baby-changing facilities (cue old joke: I swapped mine for a nice souvenir). Elsewhere, some city-centre public toilets have baby-changing areas, although these can be a bit grimy; your best bet for clean facilities is an upmarket department store. On the road, baby-changing facilities are generally bearable at motorway service stations and OK at out-of-town supermarkets.

The greatest

Some crustaceans are huge – the biggest living arthropods.

Top: Japanese spider crab display, Natural History Museum (p94), London

Bottom: Discovering ancient fossils, Lyme Regis (p264); Jurassic Coast

JOHN CANCALOSI / GETTY IMAGES ©

England

England Highlights

1 London (p66) Spending more time than you'd planned in England's (and Britain's) endlessly entertaining capital.

2 Bath (p317) Being a Jane Austen character for a day in this elegant city.

3 Lake District (p584) Wandering lonely as a cloud in the idyllic region.

4 York (p496) Exploring medieval walls, Viking sights and the soaring Gothic minster in these historic settings.

5 Falling in love with the impossibly quaint villages of the **Cotswolds** (p202).

6 Oxford (p189) Getting some higher education among the dreaming spires.

7 Cambridge (p367) Punting along the river.

8 Hadrian's Wall (p636) Seeing wild scenery and ancient engineering at this historic site.

9 Stratford-upon-Avon (p422) Catching a Shakespeare play or visiting the Bard's grave.

10 Canterbury (p153) Marvelling at one of Europe's greatest cathedrals.

London

POP 8.7 MILLION / ☑ 020 / AREA 1 569 SQ KM

Best Places to Eat

➡ Gymkhana (p125)

➡ Dinner by Heston Blumenthal (p128)

➡ Brasserie Zédel (p125)

➡ Gordon Ramsay (p128)

➡ Ledbury (p129)

Best Places to Sleep

➡ Zetter Hotel & Townhouse (p124)

➡ Citizen M (p120)

➡ Clink78 (p123)

➡ Beaumont (p119)

➡ Hoxton Hotel (p120)

Why Go?

Everyone comes to London with preconceptions shaped by a multitude of books, movies, TV shows and songs. Whatever yours are, prepare to have them exploded by this endlessly fascinating, amorphous city. You could spend a lifetime exploring it and still find that the slippery thing's gone and changed on you. One thing though is constant: that great serpent of a river enfolding the city in its sinuous loops, linking London both to the green heart of England and the world. From Roman times people from around the globe have come to London, put down roots and complained about the weather. This is one of the world's most multicultural cities – any given street yields a rich harvest of languages, and those narrow streets are also steeped in fascinating history, magnificent art, imposing architecture and popular culture. When you add an endless reserve of cool to this mix, it's hard not to conclude that London is one of the world's great cities, if not the greatest.

When to Go

London is a place that you can visit any time of the year. That said, different months and seasons boast different charms.

➡ Spring in the city sees daffodils in bloom and blossom in the trees.

➡ In June, the parks are filled with people, there's Trooping the Colour, summer arts festivals, Field Day in Victoria Park, other music events, gay pride and Wimbledon.

➡ Although the days are getting shorter, autumn in London is alive with festivals celebrating literature, the arts and culture.

➡ London in December is all about Christmas lights on Oxford and Regent Sts, and perhaps a whisper of snow.

History

London first came into being as a Celtic village near a ford across the River Thames, but the city only really took off after the Roman conquest in AD 43. The invaders enclosed their 'Londinium' in walls that still find refrain in the shape of the City (with a capital 'C') of London today.

By the end of the 3rd century AD, Londinium was home to some 30,000 people. Internal strife and relentless barbarian attacks wore the Romans down, however, and they abandoned Britain in the 5th century, reducing the settlement to a sparsely populated backwater.

The Saxons moved in next, their 'Lundenwic' prospering and becoming a large, well-organised town. As the city grew in importance, it caught the eye of Danish Vikings, who launched numerous invasions. In 1016 the Saxons, finally beaten down, were forced to accept the Danish leader Knut (Canute) as King of England, after which London replaced Winchester as capital. In 1042, the throne reverted to the Saxon Edward the Confessor, who built Westminster Abbey.

The Norman Conquest of 1066 saw William the Conqueror march into London, where he was crowned king. He built the White Tower (the core of the Tower of London), negotiated taxes with the merchants, and affirmed the city's right to self-government. From then until the late 15th century, London politics were largely taken up by a three-way power struggle between the monarchy, the Church and city guilds. An uneasy political compromise was reached between the factions, and the city expanded rapidly in the 16th century under the House of Tudor.

In a rerun of the disease that wiped out half of London's population between 1348 and 1350, the Great Plague struck in 1665, and by the time the winter cold arrested the epidemic, 100,000 Londoners had perished. The cataclysm was followed by further devastation when the Great Fire of 1666 sent the city skywards. One upshot of the conflagration was a blank canvas for master architect Sir Christopher Wren to build his magnificent churches.

Despite these setbacks, London continued to grow, and by 1700 it was Europe's largest city, with 600,000 people. An influx of foreign workers brought expansion to the east and south, while those who could afford it headed to the more salubrious environs of the north and west. Georgian London saw a surge in artistic creativity, with the likes of Dr Johnson, Handel, Gainsborough and Reynolds enriching the city's culture, while architects fashioned an elegant new metropolis.

In 1837, 18-year-old Victoria began her epic reign, as London became the fulcrum of the British Empire. The Industrial Revolution saw the building of new docks and railways (including the first underground line in 1863), while the Great Exhibition of 1851 showcased London to the world. During the Victorian era, the city's population mushroomed from just over two million to 6.6 million.

Although London suffered a relatively minor bruising during WWI, it was devastated by the Luftwaffe in WWII, when huge swaths of the centre and East End were flattened and 32,000 people were killed. Ugly housing and low-cost developments followed, and pollutants – both residential and industrial – rose steadily into the air. On 6 December 1952, the Great Smog (a lethal combination of fog, smoke and pollution) descended, killing some 4000 people.

Prosperity gradually returned to the city, and creative energy bottled up in the postwar years was suddenly unleashed. In the 'Swinging Sixties', London became the capital of cool in fashion and music – a party followed morosely by the austere 1970s. Since then the city has surfed up and down the waves of global fortunes, hanging on to its position as the world's leading financial centre.

In 2000, the modern metropolis won its first mayor of London, an elected role covering the City and all 32 urban boroughs. Bicycle-riding Boris Johnson, a Tory (Conservative) with a shock of blond hair and an affable persona, was elected in 2008, and retained his post in the 2012 mayoral election.

Triggered by the shooting of a man by police in Tottenham in August 2011, numerous London boroughs were rocked by riots characterised by looting and arson. Analysts still debate the causes of the disorder, ascribing any number of factors from single-parent families to gang culture, unemployment and criminal opportunism.

Both the Olympics and the Queen's Diamond Jubilee concocted a splendid display of pageantry for London in 2012. New overground train lines opened, a cable car was flung across the Thames and a once rundown and polluted area of East London was regenerated for the Olympic Park. The games themselves were a universally applauded success, kicked off by a stupendous Opening Ceremony orchestrated by Danny Boyle.

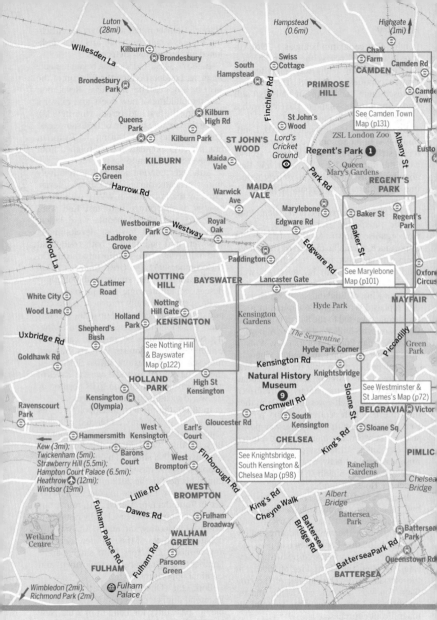

London Highlights

1 Regent's Park (p100)
Watching the world pass by in one of London's loveliest parks.

2 British Museum (p102)
Sifting through the booty of an empire at this fine museum.

3 Tower of London (p83)
Exploring the famous castle where several royals met their deaths by guillotine.

4 Westminster Abbey (p70)
Enjoying the awe-inspiring architecture at this holy spot.

5 Lamb & Flag (p134)
Raising a glass while overlooking the Thames from here or another riverside pub.

6 Shoreditch bar hop (p133)

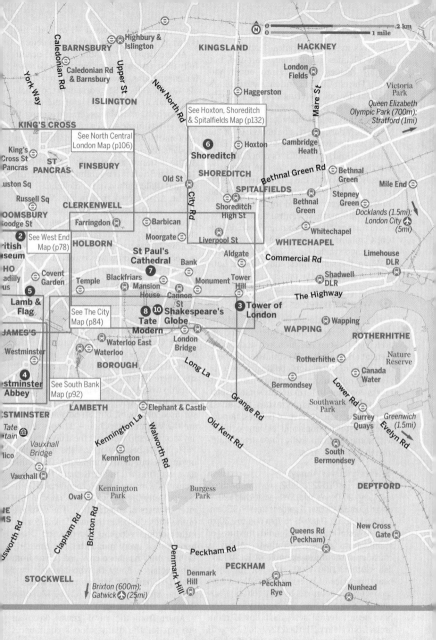

Meeting locals on a cruise around trendy Shoreditch.

❼ St Paul's Cathedral (p85) Reaching for the heavens at the top of the dome.

❽ Tate Modern (p90)

Embarking on a tour of modern and contemporary art.

❾ Natural History Museum (p94) Revelling in the astounding displays and gardens set in 5.7 hectares.

❿ Shakespeare's Globe (p140) Getting your drama fix at a Shakespearean outdoor theatre.

◉ Sights

The city's main geographical feature is the murky Thames, which snakes around, but roughly divides the city into north and south. The old City of London is the capital's financial district, covering roughly a square mile bordered by the river and the many gates of the ancient (long-gone) city walls: Newgate, Moorgate etc. The areas east of the City are collectively known as the East End. The West End, on the City's other flank, is effectively the centre of London gravity. It actually falls within the City of Westminster, one of London's 32 boroughs and long the centre of government and royalty.

Surrounding these central areas are dozens of former villages (Camden Town, Islington, Clapham etc), each with its own High St, long ago swallowed by London's sprawl.

When the sun shines, make like a Londoner and head to the parks.

◉ Westminster & St James's

Purposefully positioned outside the old City (London's fiercely independent burghers preferred to keep the monarch and parliament at arm's length), Westminster has been the centre of the nation's political power for nearly a millennium. The area's many landmarks combine to form an awesome display of authority, pomp and gravitas. St James's is an aristocratic enclave of palaces, famous hotels, historic shops and elegant edifices, with some 150 historically noteworthy buildings in its 36 hectares.

★ **Westminster Abbey**   CHURCH
(Map p72; ☑ 020-7222 5152; www.westminster-abbey.org; 20 Dean's Yard, SW1; adult/child £20/9, verger tours £5, cloister & gardens free; ⊘ 9.30am-4.30pm Mon, Tue, Thu & Fri, to 7pm Wed, to 2.30pm Sat; ◉ Westminster) A splendid mixture of architectural styles, Westminster Abbey is considered the finest example of Early English Gothic (1190–1300). It's not merely a beautiful place of worship – the Abbey also serves up the country's history cold on slabs of stone. For centuries, the country's greatest have been interred here, including 17 monarchs from Henry III (died 1272) to George II (1760). Never a cathedral (the seat of a bishop), Westminster Abbey is what is called a 'royal peculiar', administered by the Crown.

Every monarch since William the Conqueror has been crowned here, with the exception of a couple of unlucky Eds who were either murdered (Edward V) or abdicated (Edward VIII) before the magic moment.

At the heart of the Abbey is the beautifully tiled **sanctuary** (or sacrarium), a stage for coronations, royal weddings and funerals. George Gilbert Scott designed the ornate high altar in 1873. In front of the altar is the **Cosmati marble pavement** dating to 1268. It has intricate designs of small pieces of marble inlaid into plain marble, which predicts the end of the world in AD 19,693! At the entrance to the lovely **Chapel of St John the Baptist** is a sublime alabaster Virgin and Child bathed in candlelight.

The most sacred spot in the Abbey, the **shrine of St Edward the Confessor**, lies behind the high altar; access is generally restricted to protect the 13th-century flooring. St Edward was the founder of the Abbey and the original building was consecrated a few weeks before his death. His tomb was slightly altered after the original was destroyed during the Reformation but still contains Edward's remains – the only complete saint's body in Britain. Ninety-minute **verger-led tours** of the Abbey include a visit to the shrine.

The **Quire**, a sublime structure of gold, blue and red Victorian Gothic by Edward Blore, dates back to the mid-19th century. It sits where the original choir for the monks' worship would have been but bears no resemblance to the original. Nowadays, the Quire is still used for singing, but its regular occupants are the Westminster Choir – 22 boys and 12 'lay vicars' (men) who sing the daily services.

Henry III began work on the new building in 1245 but didn't complete it; the Gothic nave was finished under Richard II in 1388. Henry VII's magnificent Perpendicular Gothic-style **Lady Chapel** was consecrated in 1519 after 16 years of construction. The vestibule of the Lady Chapel is the usual place for the rather ordinary-looking **Coronation Chair**, upon which every monarch since the early 14th century has been crowned (apart from joint-monarch Mary II, who had her own chair fashioned for her coronation, which is now in the **Westminster Abbey Museum** (Map p72; ⊘ 10.30am-4pm).

Apart from the royal graves, keep an eye out for the many famous commoners interred here, especially in **Poets' Corner**, where you'll find the resting places of Chaucer, Dickens, Hardy, Tennyson, Dr Johnson and Kipling, as well as memorials to the other greats (Shakespeare, Jane Austen, Brontë

LONDON IN...

Two Days

Start in Trafalgar Sq and see at least the outside of all the big-ticket sights – London Eye, Houses of Parliament, Westminster Abbey, St James's Park and Palace, Buckingham Palace, Green Park, Hyde Park and Kensington Gardens – and then motor around the Tate Modern until you get booted out. In the evening, explore Soho. On day two, race around the British Museum, then head to the City. Start with our walking tour and finish in the Tower of London. In the evening, head to Clerkenwell for international eats, then Hoxton and Shoreditch for hip bars.

Four Days

Take the two-day itinerary but stretch it to a comfortable pace, spending extra time in the Tate Modern, British Museum and Tower of London. Stop at the National Gallery while you're in Trafalgar Sq and explore inside Westminster Abbey and St Paul's Cathedral. On your extra evenings, check out Camden and Islington or enjoy a no-expenses-spared dinner in Kensington or Knightsbridge.

One Week

Above, and add a day each for Greenwich, Kew Gardens and Hampton Court Palace.

etc). Nearby you'll find the graves of Handel and Sir Isaac Newton.

The octagonal Chapter House dates from the 1250s and was where the monks would meet for daily prayer before Henry VIII's suppression of the monasteries some three centuries later. To the right of the entrance to Chapter House is what is claimed to be the oldest door in Britain – it's been there for 950 years. Used as a treasury and 'Royal Wardrobe', the crypt-like Pyx Chamber dates from about 1070. Next door in the vaulted undercroft, the museum exhibits the death masks of generations of royalty, wax effigies representing Charles II and William III (who is on a stool to make him as tall as his wife, Mary II), armour and stained glass. Highlights are the graffiti-inscribed Mary Chair (used for the coronation of Mary II) and the Westminster Retable, England's oldest altarpiece, from the 13th century.

Parts of the Abbey complex are free to visitors. This includes the Cloister and the 900-year-old College Garden (Map p72; 10am-6pm Tue-Thu Apr-Sep, to 4pm Oct-Mar). Adjacent to the abbey is St Margaret's Church, the House of Commons' place of worship since 1614, where windows commemorate churchgoers Caxton and Milton, and Sir Walter Raleigh is buried by the altar.

In the works are the Queen's Diamond Jubilee Galleries, a new museum and gallery space located in the medieval triforium, and due to open in 2018.

⭐ Houses of Parliament   HISTORIC BUILDING
(Map p72; www.parliament.uk; Parliament Sq, SW1; Westminster) **FREE** A visit here is a journey to the heart of UK democracy. Officially called the Palace of Westminster, the Houses of Parliament's oldest part is 11th-century Westminster Hall, one of only a few sections that survived a catastrophic fire in 1834. Its roof, added between 1394 and 1401, is the earliest-known example of a hammer-beam roof. The rest is mostly a neo-Gothic confection built by Charles Barry and Augustus Pugin (1840–58).

The palace's most famous feature is its clock tower, Elizabeth Tower, aka Big Ben (Map p72; Westminster).

Ben is actually the 13.5-ton bell, named after Benjamin Hall, who was Commissioner of Works when the tower was completed in 1858.

At the business end, parliament is split into two houses. The green-hued House of Commons (Map p72; www.parliament.uk/business/commons; 2.30-10pm Mon & Tue, 11.30am-7.30pm Wed, 10.30am-6.30pm Thu, 9.30am-3pm Fri) is the lower house, where the 650 elected Members of Parliament sit. Traditionally the home of hereditary blue bloods, the scarlet-decorated House of Lords (Map p72; www.parliament.uk/business/lords; Parliament Sq, SW1; 2.30-10pm Mon & Tue, 3-10pm Wed, 11am-7.30pm Thu, 10am-close of session Fri; Westminster), with 763 members, now has peers appointed through various means. Both houses debate and vote on legislation, which is then presented to the Queen for her Royal

Westminster & St James's

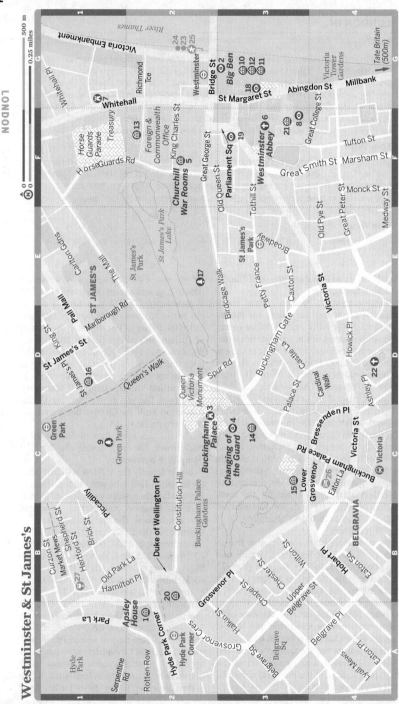

500 m
0.25 miles

River Thames

Victoria Embankment

Whitehall Pl

Whitehall

Richmond
Tce

24
23
25

Westminster
Bridge St

Big Ben
2

10
12
11

18
St Margaret St

Abingdon St

Millbank

Tate Britain
(500m)

Victoria
Tower
Gardens

Horse
Guards
Parade

Treasury

13

Foreign &
Commonwealth
Office

King Charles St

Churchill
War Rooms
5

Great George St

Parliament Sq
19

Westminster
Abbey
6

21

8

Great College St

Tufton St

Great Smith St Marsham St

Monck St

Medway St

Great Peter St

Old Pye St

Tothill St

Old Queen St

HorseGuards Rd

Horse Guards Rd

St James's Park
Lake

St James's
Park

Carlton Gdns

The Mall

ST JAMES'S

Pall Mall

King St

St James's St

St James's Pl

16

Marlborough Rd

Queen's Walk

17

Birdcage Walk

St James's
Park

Broadway

Petty France

Caxton St

Victoria St

Howick Pl

Ashley Pl

22

Victoria

Buckingham Gate

Castle La

Cardinal
Walk

Palace St

Spur Rd

Queen
Victoria
Monument

Buckingham
Palace
3

Changing of
the Guard
4

14

15

Lower
Grosvenor
Pl

Bressenden Pl

Buckingham Palace Rd

Victoria St

Eaton La

26

BELGRAVIA

Green
Park

Green
Park

9

Constitution Hill

Duke of Wellington Pl

Buckingham
Palace Gardens

Piccadilly

Curzon St

Market Mews
Shepherd St

Hertford St

Brick St

27

Old Park La

Hamilton Pl

Park La

Apsley
House
1

Hyde Park
Corner

20

Hyde Park
Corner

Grosvenor Pl

Grosvenor
Cres

Halkin St

Grosvenor St

Chapel St

Chester St

Wilton St

Upper
Belgrave St

Belgrave Pl

Hobart Pl

Eaton Sq

Belgrave Sq

Lyall Mews

Eaton Pl

Hyde
Park

Serpentine
Rd

Rotten Row

Constitution Hill

Westminster & St James's

LONDON SIGHTS

Assent (in practice, this is a formality; the last time Royal Assent was denied was in 1708). At the annual State Opening of Parliament, which takes place in May, the Queen takes her throne in the House of Lords, having arrived in the gold-trimmed Irish State Coach from Buckingham Palace (her crown travels alone in Queen Alexandra's State Coach). It's well worth lining the route for a gawk at the crown jewels sparkling in the sun.

On Saturdays year-round and on most weekdays during parliamentary recesses including Easter, summer and Christmas, visitors can join a 90-minute **guided tour** (Map p72; ☑ 020-7219 4114; www.parliament.uk/visiting/visiting-and-tours; adult/child £25.50/11) of both chambers, Westminster Hall and other historic buildings conducted by qualified Blue Badge Tourist Guides in seven languages. Afternoon tea in the Terrace Pavilion overlooking the River Thames is a popular add-on to the tours. Tour schedules change with every recess and are occasionally subject to variation or cancellation due to the State Opening of Parliament and other parliamentary business, so check ahead and book. UK residents can approach their MPs to arrange a free tour and to climb the Elizabeth Tower.

The public entrance to the Houses of Parliament is **St Stephen's Entrance** (Map p72; www.parliament.uk; Parliament Sq, SW1; ◉Westminster), housed within St Stephen's Tower.

★ **Buckingham Palace** PALACE
(Map p72; ☑ 020-7766 7300; www.royalcollection.org.uk; Buckingham Palace Rd, SW1; adult/child/child under 5 £21.50/12.30/free; ⊙ 9.30am-7.30pm

late Jul–Aug, to 6.30pm Sep; ◉ St James's Park, Victoria or Green Park) Built in 1703 for the Duke of Buckingham, Buckingham Palace replaced St James's Palace as the monarch's official London residence in 1837. When she's not delivering her trademark wave to far-flung parts of the Commonwealth, Queen Elizabeth II divides her time between here, Windsor and, in summer, Balmoral. If she's at home, the yellow, red and blue standard is flying. Some 19 lavishly furnished **State Rooms** are open to visitors when Her Royal Highness takes her holidays from late July to September.

Hung with artworks by the likes of Rembrandt, Van Dyck, Canaletto, Poussin and Vermeer, the State Rooms are open for two-hour tours that include the **Throne Room**, with his-and-hers pink chairs initialed 'ER' and 'P'. Access is by timed tickets with admission every 15 minutes (audio guide included).

From 2016, admission included access to *Fashioning a Reign: 90 Years of Style from The Queen's Wardrobe*, an exhibition affording a glimpse at royal couture during the Queen's reign.

Admission also includes access to part of the garden at Buckingham Palace as you exit, although you will have to join the three-hour State Rooms and Garden Highlights Tour (adult/child £27.50/16.40) to see the wisteria-clad Summer House and other famous features, and get an idea of the garden's full 16-hectare size.

Your ticket to Buckingham Palace is good for a return trip if bought direct from the palace ticket office (ask to have it stamped). You can even make your ticket purchase a

WILL RODRIGUES / SHUTTERSTOCK ©

1. Tower of London (p83) **2.** Windsor Castle (p225) **3.** Hampton Court Palace (p113) **4.** Buckingham Palace (p73)

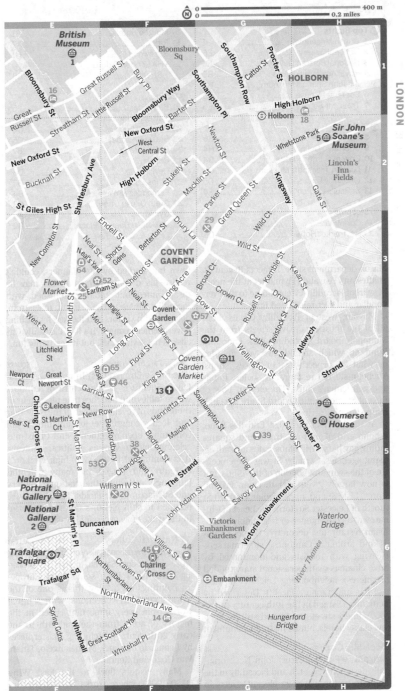

LONDON

British Museum 1

Bloomsbury Sq

Southampton Row

Procter St

Catton St

HOLBORN

Bloomsbury St

16

Great Russell St

Little Russell St

Bury Pl

Great Russell St

Southampton Pl

Barter St

High Holborn

Holborn 18

Streatham St

Bloomsbury Way

New Oxford St

West Central St

Newton St

Whetstone Park

Sir John Soane's Museum 5

New Oxford St

Shaftesbury Ave

High Holborn

Stukely St

Macklin St

Parker St

Great Queen St

Kingsway

Lincoln's Inn Fields

Bucknall St

Gate St

St Giles High St

New Compton St

Endell St

Betterton St

Drury La

29

Wild Ct

Wild St

COVENT GARDEN

Neal St

Shorts Gdns

Shelton St

Long Acre

Broad Ct

Crown Ct

Kemble St

Kean St

Drury La

Aldwych

64

Neal's Yard

52

Earlham St

Flower Market 25

Mercer St

Langley St

Neal St

Long Acre

Bow St

57

Covent Garden 21

10

Russell St

Tavistock St

Catherine St

Wellington St

Strand

West St

Litchfield St

Monmouth St

Long Acre

Floral St

James St

Covent Garden Market

11

Exeter St

9

Somerset House 6

Newport Ct

Great Newport St

Rose St

65

Garrick St

46

King St

13

Henrietta St

Southampton St

Lancaster Pl

Savoy St

Charing Cross Rd

Leicester Sq

St Martin's Crt

New Row

Bedfordbury

St Martin's La

Bedford St

Maiden La

Carting La

39

Bear St

53

38

Chandos Pl

Agar St

The Strand

Adam St

Savoy Pl

National Portrait Gallery 3

William IV St

20

John Adam St

Victoria Embankment Gardens

Victoria Embankment

Waterloo Bridge

National Gallery 2

Duncannon St

St Martin's Pl

Trafalgar Square 7

Trafalgar Sq

Northumberland St

Craven St

Villiers St

45

44

Charing Cross

Embankment

River Thames

Spring Gdns

Whitehall

Great Scotland Yd

Northumberland Ave

14

Hungerford Bridge

Whitehall Pl

N 0 — 400 m
0 — 0.2 miles

West End

◎ **Top Sights**

Mason department store. It meets Regent St, Shaftesbury Ave and Haymarket at the neon-lit swirl of Piccadilly Circus, home to the ever-popular and ever-misnamed Eros statue.

Mayfair, west of Piccadilly Circus, hogs all of the most expensive streets from the Monopoly board, including Park Lane and Bond St, which should give you an idea of what to expect: lots of pricey shops, Michelin-starred restaurants, society hotels and gentlemen's clubs. The elegant bow of Regent St and frantic Oxford St are the city's main shopping strips.

At the heart of the West End lies Soho, a boho grid of narrow streets and squares hiding gay bars, strip clubs, cafes and advertising agencies. Carnaby St was the epicentre of the swinging London of the 1960s, but is now largely given over to chain fashion stores. Lisle St and, in particular, Gerrard St (north of Leicester Sq) form the heart of Chinatown, a convergence of reasonably priced Asian restaurants, decorative Chinese arches and aromatic Cantonese supermarkets. Heaving with tourists and dominated by huge cinemas (with occasional star-studded premieres), neighbouring Leicester Sq (lester) has undergone a facelift. Described by Benjamin Disraeli in the 19th century as Europe's finest street, the Strand still boasts a few classy hotels, but its lustre has dimmed.

Piccadilly Circus   SQUARE
(Map p78; ⊖ Piccadilly Circus) John Nash originally designed Regent St and Piccadilly in the 1820s to be the two most elegant streets in

town but, curbed by city planners, couldn't realise his dream to the full. He may be disappointed, but suitably astonished, with Piccadilly Circus today: a traffic maelstrom, deluged with visitors and flanked by flashing advertisement panels. 'It's like Piccadilly Circus', as the saying goes, but it's certainly fun.

★**Trafalgar Square**   SQUARE
(Map p78; ⊖ Charing Cross) In many ways Trafalgar Square is is the centre of London, where rallies and marches take place, tens of thousands of revellers usher in the New Year and locals congregate for anything from communal open-air cinema and Christmas celebrations to various political protests. It is dominated by the 52m-high **Nelson's Column** and ringed by many splendid buildings, including the National Gallery and St Martin-in-the-Fields. The Nazis once planned to shift Nelson's Column to Berlin in the wake of a successful invasion.

★**National Gallery**   GALLERY
(Map p78; www.nationalgallery.org.uk; Trafalgar Sq, WC2; ⊗10am-6pm Sat-Thu, to 9pm Fri; ⊖ Charing Cross) **FREE** With some 2300 European paintings on display, this is one of the world's great art collections, with seminal works from every important epoch in the history of art – from the mid-13th to the early 20th century, including masterpieces by Leonardo da Vinci, Michelangelo, Titian, Van Gogh and Renoir.

Many visitors flock to the East Wing (1700–1900), where works by 18th-century

British artists such as Gainsborough, Constable and Turner, and seminal Impressionist and post-Impressionist masterpieces by Van Gogh, Renoir and Monet await.

★ **National Portrait Gallery** GALLERY
(Map p78; www.npg.org.uk; St Martin's Pl, WC2; ⊙10am-6pm Sat-Wed, to 9pm Thu & Fri; 🍴; ⊖ Charing Cross or Leicester Sq) **FREE** What makes the National Portrait Gallery so compelling is its familiarity; in many cases you'll have heard of the subject (royals, scientists, politicians, celebrities) or the artist (Andy Warhol, Annie Leibovitz, Lucian Freud). Highlights include the famous 'Chandos portrait' of William Shakespeare, the first artwork the gallery acquired (in 1856) and believed to be the only likeness made during the playwright's lifetime, and a touching sketch of novelist Jane Austen by her sister.

★ **Royal Academy of Arts** GALLERY
(Map p78; www.royalacademy.org.uk; Burlington House, Piccadilly, W1; adult/child £10/6, prices vary for exhibitions; ⊙10am-6pm Sat-Thu, to 10pm Fri; ⊖ Green Park) Britain's oldest society devoted to fine arts was founded in 1768, moving to Burlington House exactly a century later. The collection contains drawings, paintings, architectural designs, photographs and sculptures by past and present Academicians such as Joshua Reynolds, John Constable, Thomas Gainsborough, JMW Turner, David Hockney and Norman Foster.

Covent Garden Piazza SQUARE
(Map p78; ⊖ Covent Garden) London's first planned square is now mostly the preserve of visitors, who flock here to shop among the quaint old arcades, browse through eclectic market stalls and shops, cast coins at street performers pretending to be statues and traipse through the fun London Transport Museum. On the square's west side rises handsome **St Paul's Church** (www.actorschurch.org; Bedford St, WC2; ⊙8.30am-5pm Mon-Fri, varies Sat, 9am-1pm Sun; ⊖ Covent Garden), built in 1633.

London Transport Museum MUSEUM
(Map p78; www.ltmuseum.co.uk; Covent Garden Piazza, WC2; adult/child £17/free; ⊙10am-6pm Sat-Thu, 11am-6pm Fri; ⊖ Covent Garden) This entertaining and informative museum looks at how London developed as a result of better transport and contains everything from horse-drawn omnibuses, early taxis, underground trains you can drive yourself, a forward look at Crossrail (a high-frequency rail service linking Reading with east London, southeast London and Essex, due to open in 2018), plus everything in between. Check out the museum shop for imaginative souvenirs, including historical tube posters and 'Mind the Gap' socks.

★ **Sir John Soane's Museum** MUSEUM
(Map p78; www.soane.org; 13 Lincoln's Inn Fields, WC2; ⊙10am-5pm Tue-Sat, plus 6-9pm 1st Tue of month; ⊖ Holborn) **FREE** This museum is one of the most atmospheric and fascinating

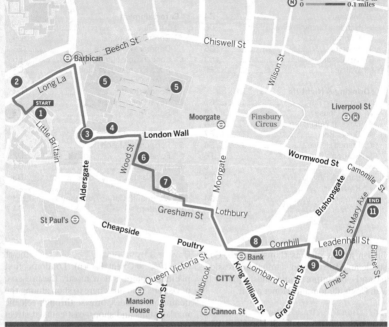

🏃 City Walk
A Taste of the City

START ST BARTHOLOMEW-THE-GREAT
END 30 ST MARY AXE (THE GHERKIN)
LENGTH 1.5 MILES; THREE HOURS

The City of London has as much history in its square mile as the rest of London put together; this walk picks out just a few of its highlights.

Start by exploring the wonderful 12th-century **①St Bartholomew-the-Great** (p87), whose atmospheric interior has been used frequently as a film set. Head through the Tudor gatehouse and turn right towards the colourful Victorian arches of **②Smithfield Market** (p87), London's last surviving meat market.

Take a right down Long Lane and another at Aldersgate St. Follow the roundabout to the right and nip up the stairs (or take the lift) to the **③Museum of London** (p86). Explore the museum's excellent galleries or head to the right to the ruins of the **④Roman city walls** and behind them the distinctive towers of the **⑤Barbican** (p142).

Turn right at Wood St to find the remaining **⑥tower of St Alban** (1698), all that's left of

a Wren-designed church destroyed in WWII bombing in 1940. Turn left into Love Lane and right into Aldermanbury – the impressive 15th-century **⑦Guildhall** (p86) is on your left. Crossing its courtyard – note the black outline of the Roman amphitheatre – continue east onto Gresham St, taking a right into Prince's St and emerging onto the busy Bank intersection lined with neoclassical temples to commerce. Behind the Duke of Wellington statue is a metal pyramid detailing the many significant buildings here.

From the **⑧Royal Exchange** (p87), follow Cornhill and take a right down Gracechurch St. Turn left into wonderful **⑨Leadenhall Market** (p146), roughly where the Roman forum once stood. As you leave the market's far end, **⑩Lloyd's of London** (p87) displays its innards for all to see. Once you turn left onto Lime St, **⑪30 St Mary Axe** (p87), or 'the Gherkin', looms before you. Built nearly 900 years after St Bartholomew-the-Great, it's tangible testimony to the city's ability to constantly reinvent itself.

in London. The building was the beautiful, bewitching home of architect Sir John Soane (1753–1837), which he left brimming with his vast architectural and archaeological collection, as well as intriguing personal effects and curiosities. The museum represents his exquisite and eccentric tastes, persuasions and proclivities.

★ **Somerset House** HISTORIC BUILDING
(Map p78; www.somersethouse.org.uk; The Strand, WC2; ⊙ galleries 10am-6pm, Safra Courtyard 7.30am-11pm; ⊜ Charing Cross, Embankment or Temple) Designed by William Chambers in 1775 for royal societies, Somerset House now contains two fabulous galleries. Near the Strand entrance, the **Courtauld Gallery** (Map p78; www.courtauld.ac.uk; Somerset House, The Strand, WC2; adult/child Tue-Sun £7/free, temporary exhibitions an additional £1.50; ⊙ 10am-6pm; ⊜ Charing Cross, Embankment or Temple) displays a wealth of 14th- to 20th-century art, including masterpieces by Rubens, Botticelli, Cézanne, Degas, Renoir, Seurat, Manet, Monet, Leger and others. Downstairs, the Embankment Galleries are devoted to temporary (mostly photographic) exhibitions; prices and hours vary.

Burlington Arcade HISTORIC BUILDING
(Map p78; www.burlington-arcade.co.uk; 51 Piccadilly, W1; ⊙ 9am-7.30pm Mon-Sat, 11am-6pm Sun; ⊜ Green Park) Flanking Burlington House, home to the Royal Academy of Arts, is this delightful arcade, built in 1819. Today it is a shopping precinct for the wealthy, and is most famous for the Burlington Berties, uniformed guards who patrol the area keeping an eye out for such offences as running, chewing gum, whistling, opening umbrellas or anything else that could lower the tone (that the arcade once served as a brothel is kept quiet).

◉ The City

With beguiling churches, hidden gardens and atmospheric lanes stuffed between iconic corporate towers and office blocks, you could spend weeks exploring the City of London, which, for most of its history, *was* London. Its boundaries have changed little since the Romans first founded their gated community here two millennia ago.

It's only in the last 250 years that the City has gone from being the very essence of London and its main population centre to just its central business district. But what a business district it is – the 'square mile' remains at the very heart of world capitalism.

Currently fewer than 10,000 people actually live here, although some 300,000 descend on it each weekday, to generate almost three-quarters of Britain's GDP before squeezing back onto the tube. On Sundays the City (capital 'C') becomes a virtual ghost town; it's nice and quiet, but come with a full stomach – most shops, eateries and pubs are closed.

★ **Tower of London** CASTLE
(Map p84; ☑ 0844 482 7777; www.hrp.org.uk/toweroflondon; Tower Hill, EC3; adult/child £25/12, audio guide £4/3; ⊙ 9am-5.30pm Tue-Sat, 10am-5.30pm Sun & Mon Mar-Oct, 9am-4.30pm Tue-Sat, 10am-4.30pm Sun & Mon Nov-Feb; ⊜ Tower Hill) The unmissable Tower of London (actually a castle of 22 towers) offers a window into a gruesome and compelling history. This was where two kings and three queens met their deaths and countless others were imprisoned. Come here to see the colourful Yeoman Warders (or Beefeaters), the spectacular Crown Jewels, the soothsaying ravens and armour fit for a *very* large king.

In the 1070s, William the Conqueror started work on the White Tower to replace the castle he'd previously had built here. By 1285, two walls with towers and a moat were built around it and the defences have barely been altered since. A former royal residence, treasury, mint and armoury, it became most famous as a prison when Henry VIII moved to Whitehall Palace in 1529 and started meting out his preferred brand of punishment.

The most striking building is the central White Tower, with its solid Norman architecture and four turrets. Today, on the entrance floor it houses a collection from the Royal Armouries, including Henry VIII's commodious suit of armour. On the 1st floor is St John's Chapel, dating from 1080 and therefore the oldest church in London. To the north stands Waterloo Barracks, which now contains the spectacular Crown Jewels, including the platinum crown of the late Queen Mother, set with the 106-carat Koh-i-Noor (Mountain of Light) diamond, and the Imperial State Crown, worn by the Queen at the State Opening of Parliament. Slow-moving travelators shunt wide-eyed visitors past the collection. On the far side of the White Tower is the Bloody Tower, where the 12-year-old Edward V and his little brother Richard were held 'for their own safety' and later murdered, perhaps by their uncle, the future Richard III. Sir Walter Raleigh

The City

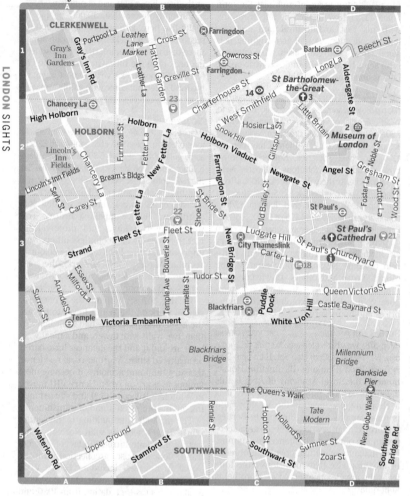

did a 13-year stretch here too under James I, when he wrote his *History of the World*.

In front of the **Chapel Royal of St Peter ad Vincula** stood Henry VIII's scaffold, where nobles such as Anne Boleyn and Catherine Howard (Henry's second and fifth wives) were beheaded. Look out for the latest in the Tower's long line of famous ravens, which legend says could cause the White Tower to collapse should they leave (their wing feathers are clipped in case they get any ideas).

To get your bearings, take the entertaining (and free) guided tour with any of the Beefeaters. Hour-long tours leave every 30 minutes from the bridge near the main entrance; the last tour is an hour before closing.

The red-brick **New Armouries Cafe** in the southeastern corner of the inner courtyard offers hot meals and sandwiches. Book online for cheaper rates for the Tower.

★ **Tower Bridge**   BRIDGE
(Map p84; ⊖ Tower Hill) London was a thriving port in 1894 when elegant Tower Bridge was built. Designed to be raised to allow ships to pass, the bridge now functions with electrical engines, replacing the original steam and hydraulic. A lift leads up from the northern

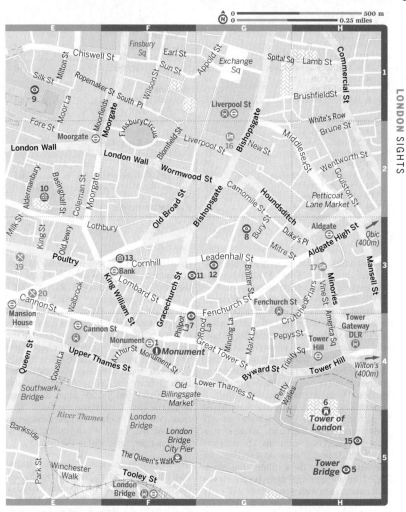

tower to the **Tower Bridge Exhibition** (Map p84; ☎020-7403 3761; www.towerbridge.org.uk; Tower Bridge, SE1; adult/child £9/3.90, incl Monument £11/5; ⊙10am-6pm Apr-Sep, 9.30am-5.30pm Oct-Mar, last admission 30min before closing; ⊝Tower Hill), where the story of its building is recounted within the upper walkway. You then walk down to the fascinating Victorian Engine Rooms, which powered the bridge lifts.

★ **St Paul's Cathedral**   CATHEDRAL
(Map p84; ☎020-7246 8350; www.stpauls.co.uk; St Paul's Churchyard, EC4; adult/child £18/8; ⊙8.30am-4.30pm Mon-Sat; ⊝St Paul's) Tower-ing over Ludgate Hill, in a superb position that's been a place of Christian worship for over 1400 years, St Paul's Cathedral is one of London's most majestic and iconic buildings. For Londoners, the vast dome, which still manages to dominate the skyline, is a symbol of resilience and pride, standing tall for more than 300 years. Viewing Sir Christopher Wren's masterpiece from the inside and climbing to the top for sweeping views of the capital is an exhilarating experience.

The cathedral was designed by Wren after the Great Fire and built between 1675 and 1710; it opened the following year. The site is

The City

ancient hallowed ground, with four other cathedrals preceding Wren's English baroque masterpiece here, the first dating from 604.

The dome, the world's second-largest cathedral dome and weighing in at 65,000 tons, is famed for sidestepping Luftwaffe incendiary bombs in the 'Second Great Fire of London' of December 1940, becoming an icon of London resilience during the Blitz. Outside the cathedral, to the north, a monument to the people of London is a simple and elegant memorial to the 32,000 Londoners killed.

Inside, some 30m above the main paved area, is the first of three domes (actually a dome inside a cone inside a dome) supported by eight huge columns. The walkway around its base, 257 steps up a staircase on the western side of the southern transept, is called the Whispering Gallery, because if you talk close to the wall, your words will carry to the opposite side, 32m away. A further 119 steps brings you to the Stone Gallery, 152 iron steps above which is the Golden Gallery at the very top, rewarded with unforgettable views of London. As part of its 300th anniversary celebrations in 2011, St Paul's underwent a £40-million renovation project that gave the church a deep clean. It's not looked this good since they cut the blue ribbon opening the cathedral in 1711.

The crypt has memorials to up to 300 heroes and military demigods, including Wellington and Nelson, whose body lies directly below the dome. But the most poignant memorial is to Wren himself. On a simple slab bearing his name, part of a Latin inscription translates as: 'If you seek his memorial, look around you'. Also here is the **Crypt Café** and the excellent Restaurant at St Paul's (p127).

Free multimedia tours lasting 1½ hours are available. Free 1½-hour guided tours leave the tour desk four times a day (typically at 10am, 11am, 1pm and 2pm); head to the desk just past the entrance to check times and book a place. Around twice a month, 60-minute tours (£8) also visit the astonishing Library, the Geometric Staircase and Great Model, and include impressive views down the nave from above the Great West Doors; check the website for dates and hours and book well ahead. Filming and photography is not permitted within the cathedral.

★ **Museum of London**   MUSEUM
(Map p84; www.museumoflondon.org.uk; 150 London Wall, EC2; ⊙10am-6pm; ⊖Barbican) `FREE`
One of the capital's best museums, this is a fascinating walk through the various incarnations of the city from Roman Londinium and Anglo-Saxon Ludenwic to 21st-century metropolis contained in two-dozen galleries. There are a lot of interactive displays with an emphasis on experience rather than learning.

Guildhall   HISTORIC BUILDING
(Map p84; ☑020-7332 1313; www.guildhall.cityof london.gov.uk; Gresham St, EC2; ⊖Bank) `FREE`
Bang in the centre of the Square Mile, Guildhall has been the City's seat of government for more than 800 years. The present building dates from the early 15th century, making it the only existing secular stone structure to have survived the Great Fire of 1666,

although it was severely damaged both then and during the Blitz of 1940.

★**Monument** TOWER
(Map p84; www.themonument.info; Junction of Fish Street Hill & Monument St, EC3; adult/child £4/2, incl Tower Bridge Exhibition £10.50/4.70; ⊙ 9.30am-6pm Apr-Sep, to 5.30pm Oct-Mar; ⊜ Monument) Sir Christopher Wren's 1677 column, known simply as the Monument, is a memorial to the Great Fire of London of 1666, whose impact on London's history cannot be overstated. An immense Doric column made of Portland stone, the Monument is 4.5m wide and 60.6m tall – the exact distance it stands from the bakery in Pudding Lane where the fire is thought to have started.

Inns of Court HISTORIC BUILDINGS
All London barristers work from within one of the four atmospheric Inns of Court, positioned between the walls of the old City and Westminster. It would take a lifetime working here to grasp all the intricacies of their arcane protocols, originating in the 13th-century. It's best just to soak up the dreamy ambience of the alleys and open spaces and thank your lucky stars you're not one of the bewigged barristers scurrying about.

★**St Bartholomew-the-Great** CHURCH
(Map p84; ☑ 020-7600 0440; www.greatstbarts. com; West Smithfield, EC1; adult/concession £5/4.50; ⊙ 8.30am-5pm Mon-Fri, 10.30am-4pm Sat, 8.30am-8pm Sun; ⊜ Farringdon or Barbican) Dating to 1123 and adjoining one of London's oldest hospitals, St Bartholomew-the-Great is one of London's most ancient churches. The authentic Norman arches and profound sense of history lend this holy space an ancient calm, while approaching from nearby Smithfield Market through the restored 13th-century half-timbered archway is like walking back in time. The church was originally part of the monastery of Augustinian Canons, but became the parish church of Smithfield in 1539 when King Henry VIII dissolved the monasteries.

Smithfield Market MARKET
(Map p84; www.smithfieldmarket.com; West Smithfield, EC1; ⊙ 2-10am Mon-Fri; ⊜ Farringdon) Smithfield is central London's last surviving meat market. Its name derives from 'smooth field', where animals could graze, although its history is far from pastoral as this was once a place where public executions were held. Visit the market by 7am at the latest to see it in full swing. The Museum of London (p86) is due to move into Smithfield Market by 2021 in a relocation costing £70 million.

Royal Exchange HISTORIC BUILDING
(Map p84; www.theroyalexchange.co.uk; Royal Exchange, EC3; ⊙ shops 10am-6pm, restaurants 8am-11pm Mon-Fri; ⊜ Bank) The Royal Exchange was founded by Thomas Gresham in 1564, and this imposing, colonnaded building at the juncture of Threadneedle St and Cornhill is the third building on the site – the first was officially opened by Elizabeth I in 1570. It ceased functioning as a financial institution in the 1980s and now houses posh shops, cafes and restaurants.

Lloyd's of London NOTABLE BUILDING
(Map p84; www.lloyds.com/lloyds/about-us/the-lloyds-building; 1 Lime St, EC3; ⊜ Aldgate or Monument) While the world's leading insurance brokers are inside underwriting everything from astronauts' lives to Mariah Carey's legs and Tom Jones' chest hair, people outside still stop to gawp at the stainless-steel external ducting, vents and staircases of this 1986 postmodern building designed by Richard Rogers, one of the architects of Paris' Pompidou Centre.

30 St Mary Axe NOTABLE BUILDING
(Gherkin; Map p84; www.30stmaryaxe.info; 30 St Mary Axe, EC3; ⊜ Aldgate) Nicknamed 'the Gherkin' for its unusual shape, 30 St Mary Axe is arguably the City's most distinctive skyscraper, dominating the skyline despite actually being slightly smaller than the neighbouring NatWest Tower. Built in 2003 by award-winning Norman Foster, the Gherkin's futuristic exterior has become an emblem of modern London – as recognisable as Big Ben and the London Eye.

◉ **South Bank**

Londoners once crossed the river to the area controlled by the licentious Bishops of Southwark for all manner of bawdy frolicking frowned upon in the City. It's a much more seemly and temperate area these days, but the frisson of theatre and entertainment survives. While South Bank only technically refers to the area of river bank between Westminster and Blackfriars Bridges (parts of which are actually on the east bank due to the way the river bends), we've used it as a convenient catch-all for those parts of Southwark and Lambeth that sit closest to the river.

Tower of London

TACKLING THE TOWER

Although it's usually less busy in the late afternoon, don't leave your assault on the Tower until too late in the day. You could easily spend hours here and not see it all. Start by getting your bearings on one of the Yeoman Warder (Beefeater) tours; they are included in the cost of admission, entertaining and the easiest way to access the **Chapel Royal of St Peter ad Vincula** ❶, which is where they finish up.

When you leave the chapel, the **Scaffold Site** ❷ is directly in front. The building immediately to your left is Waterloo Barracks, where the **Crown Jewels** ❸ are housed. These are the absolute highlight of a Tower visit, so keep an eye on the entrance and pick a time to visit when it looks relatively quiet. Once inside, take things at your own pace. Slow-moving travelators shunt you past the dozen or so crowns that are the treasury's centrepieces, but feel free to double-back for a second or even third pass.

Allow plenty of time for the **White Tower** ❹, the core of the whole complex, starting with the exhibition of royal armour. As you continue onto the 1st floor, keep an eye out for **St John's Chapel** ❺.

The famous **ravens** ❻ can be seen in the courtyard south of the White Tower. Head next through the towers that formed the **Medieval Palace** ❼, then take the **East Wall Walk** ❽ to get a feel for the castle's mighty battlements. Spend the rest of your time poking around the many other fascinating nooks and crannies of the Tower complex.

BEAT THE QUEUES

» **Buy** tickets online, avoid weekends and aim to be at the Tower first thing in the morning, when queues are shortest.

» **Become a member** An annual Historic Royal Palaces membership allows you to jump the queues and visit the Tower (and four other London palaces) as often as you like.

Chapel Royal of St Peter ad Vincula
This chapel serves as the resting place for the royals and other members of the aristocracy who were executed on the small green out front. Several other historical figures are buried here too, including Thomas More.

Dry Moat

Scaffold Site
Seven people, including three queens (Anne Boleyn, Catherine Howard and Jane Grey), lost their heads here during Tudor times, saving the monarch the embarrassment of public executions on Tower Hill. The site features a rather odd 'pillow' sculpture by Brian Catling.

Beauchamp Tower

Main Entrance

Middle Tower

Byward Tower

Bell Tower

White Tower
Much of the White Tower is taken up with an exhibition on 500 years of royal armour. Look for the virtually cuboid suit made to match Henry VIII's bloated 49-year-old body, complete with an oversized armoured codpiece to protect, ahem, the crown jewels.

St John's Chapel
Kept as plain and unadorned as it would have been in Norman times, the White Tower's 1st-floor chapel is the oldest surviving church from 1080.

Crown Jewels
When they're not being worn for ceremonies of state, Her Majesty's bling is kept here. Among the 23,578 gems, look out for the 530-carat 1st Star of Africa diamond at the top of the Sovereign's Sceptre with cross, the largest part of what was then the largest diamond ever found.

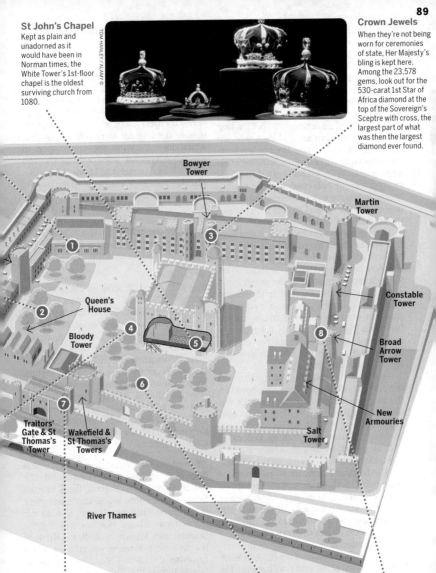

Bowyer Tower

Martin Tower

Queen's House

Bloody Tower

Constable Tower

Broad Arrow Tower

New Armouries

Salt Tower

Traitors' Gate & St Thomas's Tower

Wakefield & St Thomas's Towers

River Thames

Medieval Palace
This part of the Tower complex was begun around 1220 and was home to England's medieval monarchs. Look for the recreations of the bedchamber of Edward I (1272–1307) in St Thomas's Tower and the throne room of his father, Henry III (1216–72) in the Wakefield Tower.

Ravens
This stretch of green is where the Tower's half-dozen ravens are kept, fed on raw meat and blood-soaked biscuits. According to legend, if the ravens depart the fortress, the Tower will fall.

East Wall Walk
Follow the inner ramparts, starting from the 13th-century Salt Tower, passing through the Broad Arrow and Constable Towers, and ending at the Martin Tower, where the Crown Jewels were stored till the mid-19th century.

TOM HANLEY / ALAMY ©

CRISTIAN SANTINON / SHUTTERSTOCK ©

★ **Tate Modern**   MUSEUM

(Map p92; www.tate.org.uk; Queen's Walk, SE1; ⊙10am-6pm Sun-Thu, to 10pm Fri & Sat; 🚇📶; 🚇Blackfriars, Southwark or London Bridge) **FREE** One of London's most amazing attractions, this outstanding modern- and contemporary-art gallery is housed in the creatively revamped **Bankside Power Station** south of the Millennium Bridge. A spellbinding synthesis of modern art and capacious industrial brick design, Tate Modern has been extraordinarily successful in bringing challenging work to the masses, both through its free permanent collection and fee-paying, big-name temporary exhibitions. A stunning new extension opened in 2016, increasing the available exhibition space by 60%.

The 4.2 million bricks of the 200m-long Tate Modern is an imposing sight, designed by Swiss architects Herzog and de Meuron, who scooped the prestigious Pritzker Prize for their transformation of the empty power station. Leaving the building's central 99m-high chimney, adding a two-storey glass box onto the roof and employing the cavernous Turbine Hall as a dramatic entrance space were three huge achievements. Herzog and de Meuron also designed the new 11-storey Tate extension.

As a supreme collection of modern art, the contents of the museum are, however, the main draw. At their disposal, the curators have paintings by Georges Braque, Henri Matisse, Piet Mondrian, Andy Warhol, Mark Rothko and Jackson Pollock as well as pieces by Joseph Beuys, Damien Hirst, Claes Oldenburg and Auguste Rodin. Tate Modern's permanent collection is arranged by both theme and chronology on levels 2, 3 and 4. More than 60,000 works are on constant rotation, so if there's a particular work you would like to see, check the website to see if (and where) it's hanging.

The location is also supreme, as the ever-popular balconies on level 3 with their magnificent views of St Paul's will attest. The **Millennium Bridge** (Map p92; 🚇St Paul's or Blackfriars) elegantly conveys views direct from the Tate Modern to St Paul's Cathedral in the City on the far bank of the river. Free guided highlights tours depart at 11am, noon, 2pm and 3pm daily. Audio guides (in five languages) are available for £4 – they contain information about 50 artworks across the gallery and offer suggested tours for adults or children.

To visit the sister-museum Tate Britain, hop on the **Tate Boat** (Map p92; www.tate.org.

uk/visit/tate-boat; one-way adult/child £7.50/3.75) from Bankside Pier.

★ **Shakespeare's Globe**   HISTORIC BUILDING

(Map p92; www.shakespearesglobe.com; 21 New Globe Walk, SE1; adult/child £14/8; ⊙9am-5pm; 📶; 🚇Blackfriars, Southwark or London Bridge) Unlike other venues for Shakespearean plays, the new Globe was designed to resemble the original as closely as possible, which means having the arena open to the fickle London skies, leaving the 700 'groundlings' to stand in London's spectacular downpours. Visits to the Globe include tours of the theatre (half-hourly, generally in the morning from 9.30am, with afternoon tours on Monday too) as well as access to the exhibition space, which has fascinating exhibits about Shakespeare and theatre in the 17th century.

★ **London Eye**   VIEWPOINT

(Map p92; 🎫0871 781 3000; www.londoneye.com; adult/child £21.20/16.10; ⊙10am-8pm, to 9.30pm in summer; 🚇Waterloo) Standing 135m high in a fairly flat city, the London Eye affords views 25 miles in every direction, weather permitting. Interactive tablets provide great information (in six languages) about landmarks as they appear in the skyline. Each rotation – or 'flight' – takes a gracefully slow 30 minutes. At peak times (July, August and school holidays) it may seem like you'll spend more time in the queue than in the capsule. For £27.95, showcase your fast-track swagger.

★ **Imperial War Museum**   MUSEUM

(Map p92; www.iwm.org.uk; Lambeth Rd, SE1; ⊙10am-6pm; 🚇Lambeth North) **FREE** Fronted by a pair of intimidating 15in naval guns, this riveting museum is housed in what was the Bethlehem Royal Hospital, a psychiatric hospital also known as Bedlam. Although the museum's focus is on military action involving British or Commonwealth troops largely during the 20th century, it rolls out the carpet to war in the wider sense. Highlights include the state-of-the-art **First World War Galleries** and **Witnesses to War** in the forecourt and atrium above.

Shard   NOTABLE BUILDING

(Map p92; www.theviewfromtheshard.com; 32 London Bridge St, SE1; adult/child £30.95/24.95; ⊙10am-10pm; 🚇London Bridge) Puncturing the skies above London, the dramatic splinter-like form of the Shard has rapidly become an icon of London. The viewing platforms

TATE BRITAIN

Splendidly reopened a few years back with a stunning new art-deco-inspired staircase and a rehung collection, the older and more venerable of the two Tate siblings Tate Britain (www.tate.org.uk; Millbank, SW1; ☉10am-6pm, to 10pm 1st Fri of month; ☻Pimlico) celebrates paintings from 1500 to the present, with works from Blake, Hogarth, Gainsborough, Barbara Hepworth, Whistler, Constable and Turner, as well as vibrant modern and contemporary pieces from Lucian Freud, Francis Bacon and Henry Moore. Join a free 45-minute thematic tour (☉11am) and 15-minute Art in Focus talks (Millbank, SW1; ☉1.15pm Tue, Thu & Sat).

The stars of the show at Tate Britain are, undoubtedly, the light infused visions of JMW Turner in the Clore Gallery. After he died in 1851, his estate was settled by a decree declaring that whatever had been found in his studio – 300 oil paintings and about 30,000 sketches and drawings – would be bequeathed to the nation. The collection at the Tate Britain constitutes a grand and sweeping display of his work, including classics such as *The Scarlet Sunset* and *Norham Castle, Sunrise*.

There are also seminal works from Constable, Gainsborough and Reynolds, as well as the pre-Raphaelites, including William Holman Hunt's *The Awakening Conscience*, John William Waterhouse's *The Lady of Shalott*, *Ophelia* by John Everett Millais and Edward Burne-Jones's *The Golden Stairs*. Look out also for Francis Bacon's *Three Studies for Figures at the Base of a Crucifixion*. Tate Britain hosts the prestigious and often controversial Turner Prize for Contemporary Art from October to early December every year.

The Tate Britain also has a program of ticketed exhibitions which changes every few months; consult the website for details of the latest exhibition. The ticket office closes at 5.15pm.

on floors 68, 69 and 72 are open to the public and the views are, as you'd expect from a 244m vantage point, sweeping, but they come at a hefty price – book online at least a day in advance to save £5.

Old Operating Theatre Museum & Herb Garret
MUSEUM

(Map p92; www.thegarret.org.uk; 9a St Thomas St, SE1; adult/child £6.50/3.50; ☉10.30am-5pm; ☻London Bridge) This unique museum, 32 steps up a spiral stairway in the tower of St Thomas Church (1703), is the unlikely home of Britain's oldest operating theatre. Rediscovered in 1956, the garret was used by the apothecary of St Thomas's Hospital to store medicinal herbs. The museum looks back at the horror of 19th-century medicine – all preether, pre-chloroform and pre-antiseptic.

★ Southwark Cathedral
CHURCH

(Map p92; ☎020-7367 6700; www.cathedral.southwark.anglican.org; Montague Cl, SE1; ☉8am-6pm Mon-Fri, 9am-6pm Sat & Sun; ☻London Bridge) The earliest surviving parts of this relatively small cathedral are the retrochoir at the eastern end, which contains four chapels and was part of the 13th-century Priory of St Mary Overie, some ancient arcading by the southwest door and an arch that dates to the original Norman church. But most of the cathedral is Victorian. Inside are monuments galore, including a Shakespeare memorial. Catch evensong at 5.30pm on Tuesdays, Thursdays and Fridays, 4pm on Saturdays and 3pm on Sundays.

Design Museum
MUSEUM

(☎020-7940 8790; www.designmuseum.org; 224-238 Kensington High St, W8; ☉10am-5.45pm; ☻High St Kensington) Dedicated to popularising the importance of good design in everyday life, the Design Museum has a revolving program of special exhibitions. Past shows have ranged from Manolo Blahnik shoes to Formula One racing cars. The annual 'Design of the Year' exhibition showcases the best and latest design innovations – as the museum's tagline has it, 'Someday, the other museums will be showing this stuff'.

HMS Belfast
SHIP

(Map p92; www.iwm.org.uk/visits/hms-belfast; Queen's Walk, SE1; adult/child £14.50/7.25; ☉10am-6pm Mar-Oct, to 5pm Nov-Feb; ☻London Bridge) HMS *Belfast* is a magnet for naval-gazing kids of all ages. This large, light cruiser – launched in 1938 – served in WWII, helping to sink the German battleship *Scharnhorst*, shelling the Normandy coast on D Day and later participating in the Korean War. Its 6in guns could bombard a target 14 land miles distant. Displays offer a great insight into

South Bank

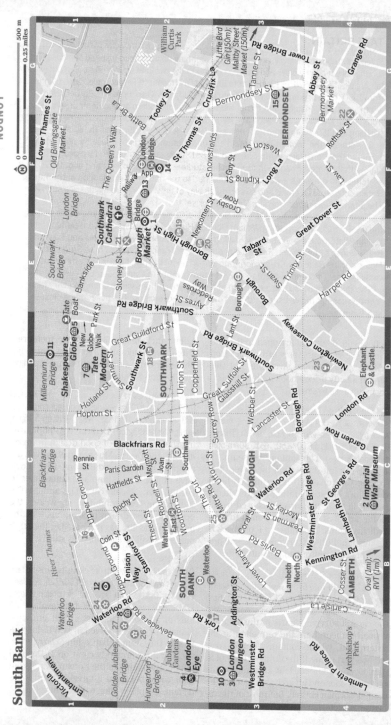

500 m
0.25 miles

Victoria Embankment

River Thames

Waterloo Bridge

Blackfriars Bridge

Golden Jubilee Bridge

Hungerford Bridge

Millennium Bridge

Upper Ground

Rennie St

Paris Garden

Hatfields St

Duchy St

Coin St

Tenison Way

Stamford St

Upper Ground

Belvedere Rd

Waterloo Rd

Cornwall Rd

Theed St

Roupell St

Joan St

Meymott St

Southwark

The Cut

Blackfriars Rd

Mitre

Ufford St

Surrey Row

Great Suffolk St

Glasshill St

Webber St

Lancaster St

Borough Rd

Union St

Copperfield St

Lant St

Great Guildford St

Southwark St

New Globe Walk

Park St

Bankside

Stoney St

Holland St

Hopton St

Sumner St

Southwark Bridge

London Bridge

Lower Thames St

Old Billingsgate Market

Tooley St

Battle Br La

The Queen's Walk

St Thomas St

Crucifix La

Tower Bridge Rd

Tanner St

Bermondsey St

Weston St

Guy St

Snowsfields

Long La

Kipling St

Crosby Row

Newcomen St

Borough High St

Borough

Redcross Way

Ayres St

Southwark Bridge Rd

Southwark Bridge Rd

Great Dover St

Tabard St

Trinity St

Swan St

Harper Rd

Newington Causeway

London Rd

Garden Row

St George's Rd

Borough Rd

Waterloo Rd

Coral St

Morley St

Pearman St

Westminster Bridge Rd

Lambeth Rd

Kennington Rd

Cosser St

Carlisle La

Lower Marsh

Bayliss Rd

Bavis Rd

Baylis Rd

Addington St

York Rd

Westminster Bridge Rd

Lambeth Palace Rd

Archbishop's Park

William Curtis Park

Bermondsey Market

Grange Rd

Abbey St

Rothsay St

Law St

Maltby Street Market (150m);
Little Bird Gin (150m)

Little Bird

BERMONDSEY

SOUTHWARK

SOUTH BANK

LAMBETH

BOROUGH

Shakespeare's Globe

Tate Modern

Southwark Cathedral

Borough Market

London Bridge

London App

Railway

London Eye

London Dungeon

Imperial War Museum

Tate Boat

Lambeth North

Waterloo

Borough

Southwark

Elephant & Castle

Oval (1mi); RVT (1mi)

Kennington

1 🏛 🔘
2 🏛
3 🔘
4 🔘
5 🏛
6 ⛪
7 🏛
8 ⛲
9 🔘
10 🔘
11 🔘
12 🔘
13 🏛
14 🔘
15 🏛
16 🔘
17 🔘
18 🔘
19 🔘
20 🔘
21 ✕
22 ✕
23 🔘
24 🔘
25 ⛲
26 🔘
27 🔘

South Bank

what life on board was like, in peace times and during military engagements.

★ **London Dungeon** HISTORIC BUILDING
(Map p92; www.thedungeons.com/london; County Hall, Westminster Bridge Rd, SE1; adult/child £28.95/24.45; ⊙10am-5pm, to 6pm Sat & Sun; ⊜Waterloo or Westminster) Older kids tend to love the London Dungeon, as the terrifying queues during school holidays and weekends testify. It's all spooky music, ghostly boat rides, macabre hangman's drop-rides, fake blood and actors dressed up as torturers and gory criminals (including Jack the Ripper and Sweeney Todd) with interactive scares galore.

London Sea Life Aquarium AQUARIUM
(Map p92; www.visitsealife.com; County Hall, Westminster Bridge Rd, SE1; adult/child £24.50/18.10; ⊙10am-7pm Mon-Fri, 9am-7pm Sat & Sun; ⊜Waterloo or Westminster) Displays look somewhat dated, but there are a couple of stand-out sights, including the shark tunnel, ray lagoon, the Gentoo penguin enclosures (penguins jump and dive at mesmerising speed) and Frozen Planet, with its flickering northern lights. Feeds and talks are scheduled throughout the day so your chances of catching one during your visit are high.

White Cube Bermondsey GALLERY
(Map p92; www.whitecube.com; 144-152 Bermondsey St, SE1; ⊙10am-6pm Tue-Sat, noon-6pm Sun; ⊜London Bridge) FREE The newest and largest of the White Cube galleries – the brainchild of Jay Jopling, dealer to the stars of the Brit Art movement who made his reputation in the 1990s by exhibiting then-unknown artists such as Damien Hirst and Antony Gormley – this gallery impresses with its large exhibition spaces, which lend themselves to monumental pieces or expansive installations using several mediums.

Hayward Gallery GALLERY
(Map p92; www.southbankcentre.co.uk; Belvedere Rd, SE1; ⊙noon-6pm Mon, 11am-7pm Tue-Wed, Sat & Sun, to 8pm Thu & Fri; ☀; ⊜Waterloo) Part of the Southbank Centre, the Hayward hosts a changing roster of contemporary art (video, installations, photography, collage, painting etc) in a 1960s Brutalist building. The gallery was closed for works at the time of research; check the website for details.

★ **Borough Market** MARKET
(Map p92; www.boroughmarket.org.uk; 8 Southwark St, SE1; ⊙10am-5pm Wed & Thu, 10am-6pm Fri, 8am-5pm Sat; ⊜London Bridge) Located here in some form or another since the 13th century (and possibly since 1014), 'London's Larder' has enjoyed an astonishing renaissance in the past 15 years. Always overflowing with food lovers, inveterate gastronomes, wide-eyed visitors and Londoners in search of inspiration for their dinner

party, this fantastic market has become firmly established as a sight in its own right. The market specialises in high-end fresh products; there are also plenty of takeaway stalls and an unreasonable number of cake stalls!

◉ Chelsea & Kensington

Known as the royal borough, Chelsea and Kensington lays claim to the highest income earners in the UK. Kensington High St has a lively mix of chains and boutiques, while even the charity shops along King's Rd resemble fashion outlets. Some of London's most beautiful and fascinating museums, clustered together in South Kensington, are must-sees come rain or shine.

★ Victoria & Albert Museum   MUSEUM
(V&A; Map p98; www.vam.ac.uk; Cromwell Rd, SW7; ◉10am-5.45pm Sat-Thu, to 10pm Fri; ⊜South Kensington) FREE The Museum of Manufactures, as the V&A was known when it opened in 1852, was part of Prince Albert's legacy to the nation in the aftermath of the successful Great Exhibition of 1851. It houses the world's largest collection of decorative arts, from Asian ceramics to Middle Eastern rugs, Chinese paintings, Western furniture, fashion from all ages and modern-day domestic appliances. The temporary exhibitions are another highlight, covering anything from David Bowie retrospectives to designer Alexander McQueen, special materials and trends.

There are more than 100 galleries in the museum, so pick carefully or join a free one-hour guided tour; there are several a day (they meet close to the information desk in the main hall) on a variety of themes including introductory tours, medieval and Renaissance tours and theatre and performance tours.

★ Natural History Museum   MUSEUM
(Map p98; www.nhm.ac.uk; Cromwell Rd, SW7; ◉10am-5.50pm; ☎; ⊜South Kensington) FREE This colossal and magnificent-looking building is infused with the irrepressible Victorian spirit of collecting, cataloguing and interpreting the natural world. The Dinosaurs Gallery (Blue Zone) is a must for children, who gawp at the animatronic T-Rex, fossils and excellent displays. Adults for their part will love the intriguing Treasures exhibition in the Cadogan Gallery (Green Zone), which houses a host of unrelated objects each telling its own unique story, from a chunk of moon rock to a dodo skeleton.

Also in the Green Zone, the Mineral Gallery is a breathtaking display of architectural perspective leading to the Vault, where you'll find the Aurora Collection of almost 300 coloured diamonds. In the Orange Zone, the vast Darwin Centre focuses on taxonomy, showcasing 28 million insects and six million plants in a giant cocoon; glass windows allow you to watch scientists at work.

At the centre of the museum is Hintze Hall, which resembles a cathedral nave – quite fitting for a time when the natural sciences were challenging the biblical tenets of Christian orthodoxy. The hall is dominated by the over-arching cast of a Diplodocus skeleton (nicknamed Dippy), which is due to be replaced by the real skeleton of a diving blue whale (*Balaenoptera musculus*), hung from the ceiling, in 2017.

A slice of English countryside in SW7, the beautiful Wildlife Garden next to the West Lawn encompasses a range of British lowland habitats, including a meadow with farm gates and a bee tree where a colony of honey bees fills the air.

In 2018, the eastern grounds are also due to be redesigned to feature a geological and palaeontological walk, with a bronze sculpture of Dippy as well as ferns and cycads.

The entire museum and its gardens cover a huge 5.7 hectares and contains 80 million specimens from across the natural world. More than five million visitors come each year, so queues can sometimes get long, especially during the school holidays.

★ Science Museum   MUSEUM
(Map p98; www.sciencemuseum.org.uk; Exhibition Rd, SW7; ◉10am-6pm; ☎; ⊜South Kensington) FREE With seven floors of interactive and educational exhibits, this scientifically spellbinding museum will mesmerise adults and children alike, covering everything from early technology to space travel. A perennial favourite is Exploring Space, a gallery featuring genuine rockets and satellites and a full-size replica of the 'Eagle', the lander that took Neil Armstrong and Buzz Aldrin to the moon in 1969. The Making the Modern World Gallery next door is a visual feast of locomotives, planes, cars and other revolutionary inventions.

The fantastic Information Age Gallery on level 2 showcases how information and communication technologies – from the telegraph to smartphones – have transformed our lives since the 19th century. Standout displays include wireless sent by a sinking

Titanic, the first BBC radio broadcast and a Soviet BESM 1965 super-computer. Also on level 2 is Media Space, a gallery dedicated to excellent photographic exhibitions from the National Photography Collection (adult/child £8/free).

The 3rd-floor Flight Gallery (free tours 1pm most days) is a favourite place for children, with its gliders, hot-air balloons and aircraft, including the Gipsy Moth, which Amy Johnson flew to Australia in 1930. This floor also features a Red Arrows 3D flight simulation theatre (adult/children £6/5) and Fly 360-degree flight-simulator capsules (£12 per capsule). Launchpad, on the same floor, is stuffed with (free) hands-on gadgets exploring physic and the properties of liquids.

Glimpses of Medical History on level 4 isn't as high-tech as the rest of the museum but is highly evocative with models and life-size reconstructions showing how medicine – from childbirth to dentistry – was practised through the ages.

If you've kids under the age of five, pop down to the basement and the Garden, where there's a fun-filled play zone, including a water-play area, besieged by tots in orange waterproof smocks.

★ Hyde Park   PARK

(Map p98; www.royalparks.org.uk/parks/hyde-park; ⊙ 5am-midnight; ⊜ Marble Arch, Hyde Park Corner or Queensway) At 145 hectares, Hyde Park is central London's largest open space, expropriated from the Church in 1536 by Henry VIII and turned into a hunting ground and later a venue for duels, executions and horse racing. The 1851 Great Exhibition was held here, and during WWII the park became an enormous potato field. These days, there's boating on the Serpentine, summer concerts (Bruce Springsteen, Florence + The Machine, Patti Smith), film nights and other warm-weather events.

★ Kensington Palace   PALACE

(Map p122; www.hrp.org.uk/kensingtonpalace; Kensington Gardens, W8; adult/child £16.30/free; ⊙ 10am-6pm Mar-Oct, to 5pm Nov-Feb; ⊜ High St Kensington) Built in 1605, the palace became the favourite royal residence under William and Mary of Orange in 1689, and remained so until George III became king and relocated to Buckingham Palace. Today, it is still a royal residence, with the likes of the Duke and Duchess of Cambridge (Prince William and his wife Catherine) and Prince Harry

living there. A large part of the palace is open to the public, however, including the King's and Queen's State Apartments.

Kensington Gardens   PARK

(Map p122; www.royalparks.org.uk/parks/kensington-gardens; ⊙ 6am-dusk; ⊜ Queensway or Lancaster Gate) Kensington Gardens is a gorgeous collection of manicured lawns, tree-shaded avenues and basins immediately west of Hyde Park. The picturesque 107-hectare expanse is technically part of Kensington Palace, located in the far west of the gardens. The large Round Pond is enjoyable to amble around and also worth a look are the lovely fountains in the Italian Gardens (Map p98; Kensington Gardens; ⊜ Lancaster Gate), believed to be a gift from Albert to Queen Victoria.

Albert Memorial   MONUMENT

(Map p98; ☑ tours 020-8969 0104; Kensington Gardens; tours adult/concession £8/7; ⊙ tours 2pm & 3pm 1st Sun of month Mar-Dec; ⊜ Knightsbridge or Gloucester Rd) This splendid Victorian confection on the southern edge of Kensington Gardens is as ostentatious as its subject. Purportedly humble, Queen Victoria's German husband Albert (1819–61) insisted he did not want a monument. Ignoring the good prince's wishes, the Lord Mayor instructed George Gilbert Scott to build the 53m-high, gaudy Gothic memorial – the 4.25m-tall gilded statue of the prince, surrounded by 187 figures representing the continents (Asia, Europe, Africa and America), the arts, industry and science, went up in 1876.

Saatchi Gallery   GALLERY

(Map p98; www.saatchigallery.com; Duke of York's HQ, King's Rd, SW3; ⊙ 10am-6pm; ⊜ Sloane Sq) FREE This enticing gallery hosts temporary exhibitions of experimental and thought-provoking work across a variety of media. The white and sanded bare-floorboard galleries are magnificently presented, but save some wonder for Gallery 15, where Richard Wilson's *20:50* is on permanent display. Mesmerising, impassive and ineffable, it's a riveting tour de force. A cool shop chips in on the 1st floor.

Royal Hospital Chelsea   HISTORIC BUILDINGS

(Map p98; www.chelsea-pensioners.co.uk; Royal Hospital Rd, SW3; ⊙ grounds 10am-4.30pm Mon-Sat, Great Hall shuts daily noon to 2pm, museum 10am-4pm Mon-Fri; ⊜ Sloane Sq) FREE Designed by Christopher Wren, this superb structure was built in 1692 to provide shelter for ex-servicemen. Since the reign of Charles

Victoria & Albert Museum

HALF-DAY HIGHLIGHTS TOUR

The art- and design-packed V&A is vast: we have devised an easy-to-follow tour of the museum highlights to help cover some signature pieces while also allowing you to appreciate some of the grandeur of the museum architecture.

Enter the V&A by the Grand Entrance off Cromwell Rd and immediately turn left to explore the Islamic Middle East Gallery and to discover the sumptuous silk-and-wool **Ardabil Carpet ❶**. Among the pieces from South Asia in the adjacent gallery is the terrifying automated **Tipu's Tiger ❷**. Continue to the outstanding **Fashion Gallery ❸** with its displays of clothing styles through the ages. The magnificent gallery opposite houses the **Raphael Cartoons ❹**, large paintings by Raphael used to weave tapestries for the Vatican. Take the stairs to Level 2 and the Britain 1500–1760 Gallery; turn left in the

Raphael Cartoons
These seven drawings by Raphael, depicting the acts of St Peter and St Paul, were the full-scale preparatory works for seven tapestries that were woven for the Sistine Chapel in the Vatican.

Fashion Gallery
With clothing from the 18th century to the present day, this circular and chronologically arranged gallery showcases evening wear, undergarments and iconic fashion milestones, such as 1960s dresses designed by Mary Quant.

The Great Bed of Ware
Created during the reign of Queen Elizabeth I, its headboard and bedposts are etched with ancient graffiti; the 16th-century oak Great Bed of Ware is famously name-dropped in Shakespeare's *Twelfth Night*.

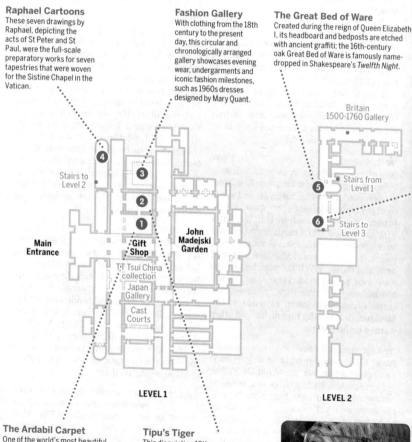

Britain 1500-1760 Gallery

Stairs to Level 2

Stairs from Level 1

Stairs to Level 3

Main Entrance

Gift Shop

John Madejski Garden

Tsui China collection

Japan Gallery

Cast Courts

LEVEL 1

LEVEL 2

The Ardabil Carpet
One of the world's most beautiful carpets, the Ardabil was completed in 1540, one of a pair commissioned by Shah Tahmasp, ruler of Iran. The piece is most astonishing for the artistry of the detailing and the subtlety of design.

Tipu's Tiger
This disquieting 18th-century wood-and-metal mechanical automaton depicts a European being savaged by a tiger. When a handle is turned, an organ hidden within the feline mimics the cries of the dying man, whose arm also rises.

gallery to find the **Great Bed of Ware** ❺, beyond which rests the exquisitely crafted artistry of **Henry VIII's Writing Box** ❻. Head up the stairs into the Metalware Gallery on Level 3 for the **Hereford Screen** ❼. Continue through the Ironwork and Sculpture Galleries and through the Leighton Corridor to the glittering **Jewellery Gallery** ❽. Exit through the Stained Glass gallery, at the end of which you'll find stairs back down to level 1.

TOP TIPS

» **More Info** Museum attendants are always at hand along the route.

» **Photography** Allowed in most galleries, except the Jewellery Gallery, the Raphael Cartoons and in exhibitions.

» **Evening Exploration** Avoid daytime crowds: visit the V&A till 10pm on Friday.

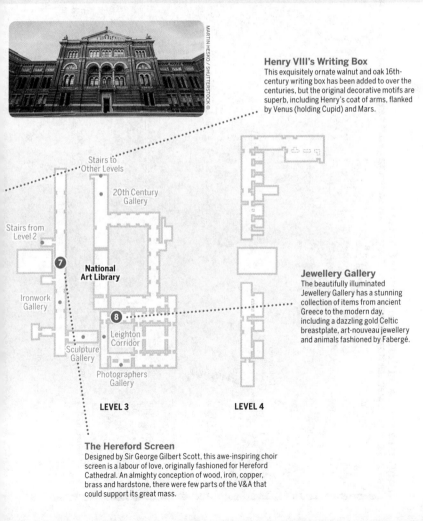

MARTIN HESKO / SHUTTERSTOCK ©

Henry VIII's Writing Box
This exquisitely ornate walnut and oak 16th-century writing box has been added to over the centuries, but the original decorative motifs are superb, including Henry's coat of arms, flanked by Venus (holding Cupid) and Mars.

Stairs to
Other Levels

20th Century
Gallery

Stairs from
Level 2

❼

**National
Art Library**

Ironwork
Gallery

❽

Leighton
Corridor

Sculpture
Gallery

Photographers
Gallery

LEVEL 3

LEVEL 4

Jewellery Gallery
The beautifully illuminated Jewellery Gallery has a stunning collection of items from ancient Greece to the modern day, including a dazzling gold Celtic breastplate, art-nouveau jewellery and animals fashioned by Fabergé.

The Hereford Screen
Designed by Sir George Gilbert Scott, this awe-inspiring choir screen is a labour of love, originally fashioned for Hereford Cathedral. An almighty conception of wood, iron, copper, brass and hardstone, there were few parts of the V&A that could support its great mass.

LONDON

Knightsbridge, South Kensington & Chelsea

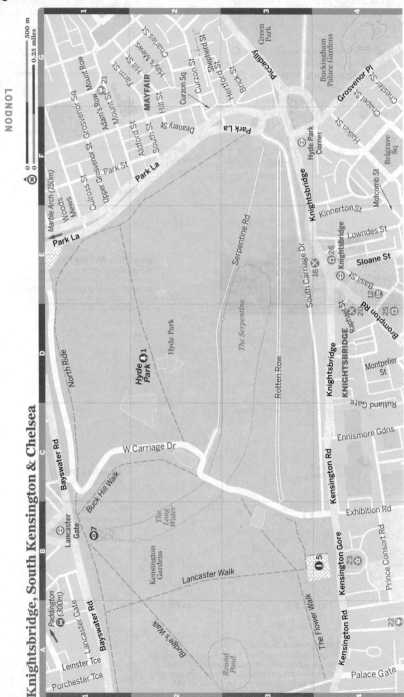

0 | 500 m
0 | 0.25 miles

Marble Arch (150m)

Paddington (300m)

Leinster Tce
Porchester Tce
Lancaster Gate
Bayswater Rd
Lancaster Gate
Bayswater Rd

Woods Mews
Culross St
Upper Grosvenor St
Park St
Grosvenor Sq
Adam's Row
Mount Row
Mount St
Hill St
Farm St
Aldford St
South St
Deanery St
Park La

Curzon Sq
Curzon St
Hay's Mews
Charles St
Hill St
Shepherd St
Hertford St
Brick St
Piccadilly

MAYFAIR

21

Park La
Park La

Green Park

Buckingham Palace Gardens
Grosvenor St
Chapel St
Chester St
Halkin St
Belgrave Sq
Hyde Park Corner
Knightsbridge
Kinnerton St
Lowndes St
Motcomb St

North Ride

Hyde Park

Hyde Park 1

The Serpentine
Serpentine Rd

The Long Water
Buck Hill Walk

Kensington Gardens

Lancaster Walk

Budge's Walk

Round Pond

The Flower Walk

Bayswater Rd

W. Carriage Dr

Rotten Row

South Carriage Dr

Knightsbridge
KNIGHTSBRIDGE
Rutland Gate
Montpelier St

Sloane St
Basil St
Knightsbridge
16
26
Brompton Rd
Raphael St
20
12
25

Ennismore Gdns

Exhibition Rd

Kensington Rd

Kensington Gore

Kensington Rd
Kensington Rd

Prince Consort Rd

Palace Gate

23

22

5

7

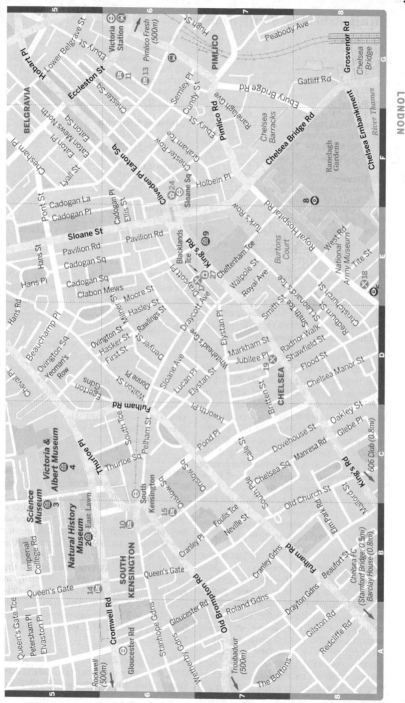

Knightsbridge, South Kensington & Chelsea

II, it has housed hundreds of war veterans, known as Chelsea Pensioners. They're fondly regarded as national treasures, and cut striking figures in the dark-blue greatcoats (in winter) or scarlet frock coats (in summer) that they wear on ceremonial occasions.

Chelsea Physic Garden   GARDENS
(Map p98; www.chelseaphysicgarden.co.uk; 66 Royal Hospital Rd, SW3; adult/child £9.50/6.95; ☉11am-6pm Tue-Fri & Sun Apr-Oct, 9.30am-4pm Mon-Fri Nov-Mar; ⊖ Sloane Sq) This walled pocket of botanical enchantment was established by the Apothecaries' Society in 1673 for students working on medicinal plants and healing. One of Europe's oldest of its kind, the small grounds are a compendium of botany, from carnivorous pitcher plants to rich yellow flag irises, a cork oak from Portugal, the largest outdoor fruiting olive tree in the British Isles, rare trees and shrubs. The site, not far from the river, ensures a slightly warmer microclimate to protect nonnative plants.

Fulham Palace   HISTORIC BUILDING
(www.fulhampalace.org; Bishop's Ave, SW6; ☉palace 12.30-4.30pm Mon-Thu, noon-5pm Sun summer, slightly earlier hours in winter, gardens dawn-dusk daily; ⊖ Putney Bridge) FREE Within stumbling distance of the Thames, this summer home of the bishops of London from 704 to 1975 is an appealing blend of architectural styles immersed in beautiful gardens and, until 1924, when filled with rubble, enclosed by the longest moat in England. The oldest surviving palace chunk

is the little red-brick Tudor gateway, while the main building dates from the mid-17th century, remodelled in the 19th century.

◎ Marylebone

Not as exclusive as its southern neighbour Mayfair, hip Marylebone has one of London's most pleasant high streets and the famous, if rather disappointing, Baker St, immortalised in the hit song by Gerry Rafferty and strongly associated with Victoria-era sleuth Sherlock Holmes (there's a museum and gift shop at his fictional address, 221b).

Regent's Park   PARK
(www.royalparks.org.uk; ☉5am-9.30pm; ⊖Regent's Park) The most elaborate and formal of London's many parks, Regent's Park is one of the capital's loveliest green spaces. Among its many attractions are London Zoo (p100), Regent's Canal, an ornamental lake and sports pitches where locals meet to play football, rugby and volleyball. Queen Mary's Gardens, towards the south of the park, are particularly pretty, especially in June when the roses are in bloom. Performances take place here in an open-air theatre (☎0844 826 4242; www.openairtheatre.org; Queen Mary's Gardens, NW1; ☉May-Sep; ⊖Baker St) during summer.

★ZSL London Zoo   ZOO
(Map p131; www.londonzoo.co.uk; Outer Circle, Regent's Park, NW1; adult/child £25.50/18.50;

Marylebone

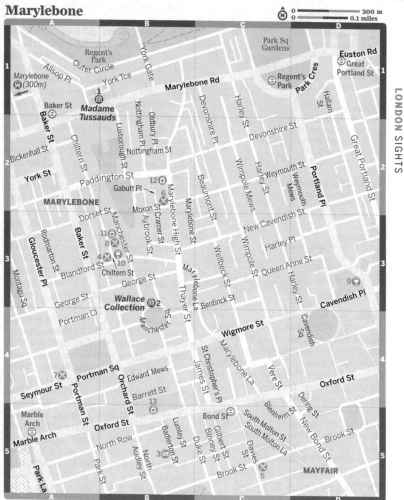

⊙ 10am-6pm Mar-Sep, to 5pm Oct, to 4pm Nov-Feb; 🚇 274) Established in 1828, these 15-hectare zoological gardens are among the oldest in the world. The emphasis nowadays is firmly placed on conservation, education and breeding. Highlights include Penguin Beach, Gorilla Kingdom, Tiger Territory, the walk-through In with the Lemurs, In with the Spiders and Meet the Monkeys. Land of the Lions is a new enclosure to house its Asiatic lions. Feeding sessions and talks take place throughout the day – join in with a spot of afternoon tea (adults/children £19.75/10).

Regent's Canal CANAL

(Map p131) To escape the crowded streets and enjoy a picturesque, waterside angle on North London, take to the canals that once played such a vital role in the transport of goods across the capital. The towpath of the Regent's Canal also makes an excellent shortcut across North London, either on foot or by bike. In full, the ribbon of water runs 9 miles from Little Venice (where it connects with the Grand Union Canal) to the Thames at Limehouse.

Marylebone

⦿ Top Sights

🛏 Sleeping

✗ Eating

◉ Drinking & Nightlife

⦿ Shopping

★**Madame Tussauds**　　　　　　MUSEUM

(Map p101; ☏0870 400 3000; www.madame-tussauds.com/london; Marylebone Rd, NW1; adult/child £35/29.50; ⊙8.30am-6pm Mon-Thu, 9am-6pm Fri-Sun; ⊖Baker St) It may be kitschy and pricey (book online for much cheaper rates), but Madame Tussauds makes for a fun-filled day. There are photo ops with your dream celebrity (Daniel Craig, Miley Cyrus, Audrey Hepburn, the Beckhams), the Bollywood gathering (studs Hrithik Roshan and Salman Khan) and the Royal Appointment (the Queen, Harry, William and Kate).

⦿ Bloomsbury & St Pancras

With the University of London and British Museum within its genteel environs, it's little wonder that Bloomsbury has attracted a lot of very clever, bookish people over the years. Between the world wars, these pleasant streets were colonised by a group of artists and intellectuals known collectively as the Bloomsbury Group, which included novelists Virginia Woolf and EM Forster and the economist John Maynard Keynes. Russell Sq, its very heart, was laid out in 1800 and is one of London's largest and loveliest.

★**British Museum**　　　　　　MUSEUM

(Map p78; ☏020-7323 8299; www.britishmuseum.org; Great Russell St, WC1; ⊙10am-5.30pm Sat-Thu,

to 8.30pm Fri; ⊖Russell Sq or Tottenham Court Rd) **FREE** The country's largest museum and one of the world's oldest and finest, this famous museum boasts vast Egyptian, Etruscan, Greek, Roman, European and Middle Eastern galleries, among others. It is frequently London's most-visited attraction, drawing more than six million visitors annually.

Don't miss the Rosetta Stone, the key to deciphering Egyptian hieroglyphics, discovered in 1799; the controversial Parthenon Sculptures, taken from the Parthenon in Athens by Lord Elgin (the British ambassador to the Ottoman Empire); and the large collection of Egyptian mummies. Other must-sees include the Anglo-Saxon Sutton Hoo burial relics and the Winged Bulls from Khorsabad.

Begun in 1753 with a 'cabinet of curiosities' sold to the nation by royal physician Sir Hans Sloane, the collection mushroomed over the ensuing years partly through acquisitions, bequests and plundering the empire. The grand Enlightenment Gallery was the first section of the redesigned museum to be built in the 1820s.

The Great Court, restored and augmented by Norman Foster in 2000, has a spectacular glass-and-steel roof, making it one of the most impressive architectural spaces in the capital. In the centre is the Reading Room, with its stunning blue-and-gold domed ceiling made of papier mâché, where Karl Marx researched and wrote *Das Kapital*.

The British Museum's extension, the £135 million World Conservation and Exhibitions Centre in its northwestern corner, opened in 2014, in the same year as the Sainsbury Exhibitions Gallery, which hosts high-profile exhibitions.

The museum is huge, so make a few focused visits if you have time, and consider taking one of the free tours. There are 15 free 30- to 40-minute eye-opener tours of individual galleries per day. The museum also has free daily gallery talks, a highlights tour (adult/child £12/free, 11.30am and 2pm Friday, Saturday and Sunday), free 45-minute lunchtime gallery talks (1.15pm Tuesday to Friday) and free 20-minute spotlight tours on Friday evenings. Audio guides (£5) can be found at the audio-guide desk in the Great Court.

★**British Library**　　　　　　LIBRARY

(Map p106; www.bl.uk; 96 Euston Rd, NW1; ⊙galleries 9.30am-6pm Mon & Fri, 9.30am-5pm Sat, 9.30am-8pm Tue-Thu, 11am-5pm Sun; ☏; ⊖King's

LOCAL KNOWLEDGE

FREE LONDON

Natural History Museum (p94) Every British child visits this building at least once, and so should you.

Tate Modern (p90) Hosts art designed to perplex and enthral.

Victoria & Albert Museum (p94) It's not overstating it to say that this is the world's greatest art-and-design museum.

National Gallery (p80) One of the world's great art collections, with some 2300 European paintings on display.

Hyde Park (p95) Millions of people come to sunbathe, boat, swim and picnic around the Serpentine, or to hear soapbox oratory at Speaker's Corner.

Science Museum (p94) Seven floors of interactive and educational exhibits.

Wallace Collection (Map p101; www.wallacecollection.org; Hertford House, Manchester Sq, W1; ⊙10am-5pm; ⊖Bond St) An enthralling glimpse into 18th-century aristocratic life.

Grant Museum of Zoology (Map p106; www.ucl.ac.uk/museums/zoology; Rockefeller Building, University College London, 21 University St, WC1; ⊙1-5pm Mon-Sat; ⊖Euston Sq) Collects 68,000 specimens from around the animal kingdom.

Highgate Cemetery (p112) London's most famous graveyard is also a de facto nature reserve.

Tate Britain (p91) Displays paintings from 1500 to the present; the works of JMW Turner are a particular highlight.

Regent's Park (p100) One of the city's most pleasant green spaces.

Wellcome Collection (p103) Celebrates the intersection of art, science and medicine.

Hampstead Heath (p112) Woodlands and meadows sprawled across 320 hectares.

Cross St Pancras) **FREE** Consisting of low-slung red-brick terraces and fronted by a large plaza featuring an oversized statue of Sir Isaac Newton, Colin St John Wilson's British Library building is a love-it-or-hate-it affair (Prince Charles likened it to a secret-police academy). Completed in 1997, it's home to some of the greatest treasures of the written word, including the *Codex Sinaiticus* (the first complete text of the New Testament), Leonardo da Vinci's notebooks and a copy of the Magna Carta (1215).

★**Wellcome Collection** MUSEUM
(Map p106; www.wellcomecollection.org; 183 Euston Rd, NW1; ⊙10am-6pm Tue, Wed & Fri-Sun, to 10pm Thu; ⊖Euston Sq) **FREE** Focusing on the interface of art, science and medicine, this clever and resourceful museum is fascinating. There are interactive displays where you can scan your face and watch it stretched into the statistical average, wacky modern sculptures inspired by various medical conditions, and downright creepy things, such as an actual cross-section of a body and enlargements of parasites (fleas, body lice, scabies) to terrifying proportions.

Charles Dickens Museum MUSEUM
(Map p106; www.dickensmuseum.com; 48 Doughty St, WC1; adult/child £9/4; ⊙10am-5pm, last admission 4pm; ☎; ⊖Chancery Lane or Russell Sq) A £3.5-million renovation made this museum, located in a handsome four-storey house that was the great Victorian novelist's sole surviving residence in London, bigger and better than ever. A period kitchen in the basement and a nursery in the attic were added, and newly acquired 49 Doughty St increased the exhibition space substantially.

⊙ Hoxton, Shoreditch & Spitalfields

These revitalised and hip areas northeast of the City have enough sightseeing allure to keep daytime travellers occupied, but things really get going in the evening, when the late-night pubs, clubs and restaurants come into their own. Vibrant Hoxton and Shoreditch form the centre of gravity for nightlife, while Sunday is optimum for strolling leisurely through Spitalfields after a Saturday night out. Over the centuries, waves of immigrants have left their mark here, and it's

The British Museum

A HALF-DAY TOUR

The British Museum, with almost eight million items in its permanent collection, is so vast and comprehensive that it can be daunting for the first-time visitor. To avoid a frustrating trip – and getting lost on the way to the Egyptian mummies – set out on this half-day exploration, which takes in some of the museum's most important sights. If you want to see and learn more, join a tour or grab an audioguide (£5).

A good starting point is the **Rosetta Stone ❶**, the key that cracked the code to ancient Egypt's writing system. Nearby treasures from Assyria – an ancient civilisation centred in Mesopotamia between the Tigris and Euphrates Rivers – including the colossal **Khorsabad Winged Bulls ❷**, give way to the **Parthenon Sculptures ❸**, highpoints of classical Greek art that continue to influence us today. Be sure to see both the sculptures and the monumental frieze celebrating the birth of

Winged Bulls from Khorsabad
This awesome pair of alabaster winged bulls with human heads once guarded the entrance to the palace of Assyrian King Sargon II at Khorsabad in Mesopotamia, a cradle of civilisation in present-day Iraq.

Parthenon Sculptures
The Parthenon, a white marble temple dedicated to Athena, was part of a fortified citadel on the Acropolis in Athens. There are dozens of sculptures and friezes with models and interactive displays explaining how they all once fitted together.

Ancient Greece & Rome ❸

Lion Hunt Reliefs from Nineveh ❷

West Stairs

❶ ❹

South Stairs

Main Entrance

Great Court

Reading Room

Great Court Shop

China, India & Southeast Asia

North America

Ticket Desk (Temporary Exhibitions)

GROUND FLOOR

Rosetta Stone
Written in hieroglyphic, demotic (cursive ancient Egyptian script used for everyday use) and Greek, the 762kg stone contains a decree exempting priests from tax on the first anniversary of young Ptolemy V's coronation.

Bust of Ramesses the Great
The most impressive sculpture in the Egyptian galleries, this 7.5-tonne bust portrays Ramesses II, scourge of the Israelites in the Book of Exodus, as great benefactor.

VISITBRITAIN / JAMES MCCORMICK / GETTY IMAGES ©

FUTURE LIGHT / GETTY IMAGES ©

Athena. En route to the West Stairs is a huge bust of **Pharaoh Ramesses II** ❹, just a hint of the large collection of **Egyptian mummies** ❺ upstairs. (The earliest, affectionately called Ginger because of wispy reddish hair, was preserved simply by hot sand.) The Romans introduce visitors to the early Britain galleries via the rich **Mildenhall Treasure** ❻. The Anglo-Saxon **Sutton Hoo Ship Burial** ❼ and the medieval **Lewis Chessmen** ❽ follow.

EATING OPTIONS

» **Court Cafes** At the northern end of the Great Court; takeaway counters with salads and sandwiches; communal tables

» **Gallery Cafe** Slightly out of the way near Room 12; quieter; offers hot dishes

» **Court Restaurant** Upstairs overlooking the former Reading Room; sit-down meals

Lewis Chessmen
The much-loved 78 chess pieces portray faceless pawns, worried-looking queens, bishops with their mitres turned sideways and rooks as 'warders', gnawing away at their shields.

FEARGUS COONEY / GETTY IMAGES ©

Egyptian Mummies
Among the rich collection of mummies and funerary objects is 'Ginger', who was buried at the site of Gebelein, in Upper Egypt, more than 5000 years ago, and Katebet, a one-time chantress (ritual performer) at the Amun temple in Karnak.

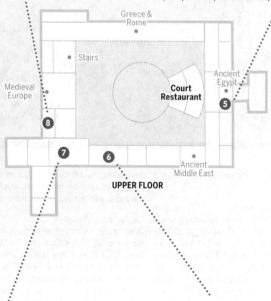

Greece & Rome

Stairs

Medieval Europe

Ancient Egypt

Court Restaurant

❺

❽

❼

❻

Ancient Middle East

UPPER FLOOR

Sutton Hoo Ship Burial
This unique grave of an important (but unidentified) Anglo-Saxon royal has yielded drinking horns, gold buckles and a stunning helmet with face mask.

Mildenhall Treasure
Roman gods such as Neptune and Bacchus share space with early Christian symbols like the *chi-rho* (short for 'Christ') on the find's three dozen silver bowls, plates and spoons.

North Central London

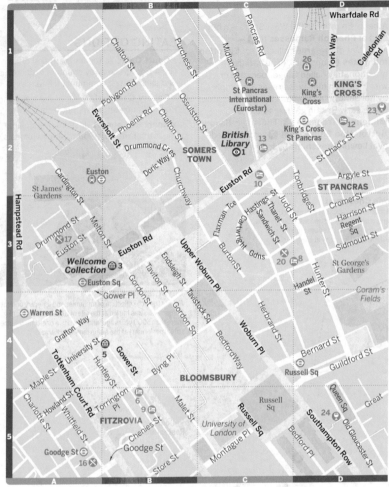

a great place to come for diverse cuisine and vibrant nightlife.

★ **Dennis Severs' House**   MUSEUM
(Map p132; ☑ 020-7247 4013; www.dennissevers house.co.uk; 18 Folgate St, E1; day/night £10/15; ☺ noon-2pm & 5-9pm Mon, 5-9pm Wed & Fri, noon-4pm Sun; ☻ Shoreditch High St) This extraordinary Georgian House is set up as if its occupants – a family of Huguenot silk weavers – had just walked out the door. There are half-drunk cups of tea and partially consumed food, lit candles and, in perhaps unnecessary attention to detail, a full chamber pot by the

bed. More than a museum, it's an opportunity to meditate on the minutiae of everyday Georgian life through silent exploration.

★ **Geffrye Museum**   MUSEUM
(Map p132; www.geffrye-museum.org.uk; 136 Kingsland Rd, E2; ☺ 10am-5pm Tue-Sun; ☻ Hoxton) **FREE** If you like nosing around other people's homes, you'll love this museum, entirely devoted to middle-class domestic interiors. Built in 1714 as a home for poor pensioners, these beautiful ivy-clad brick almshouses have been converted into a series of living rooms, dating from 1630 to the

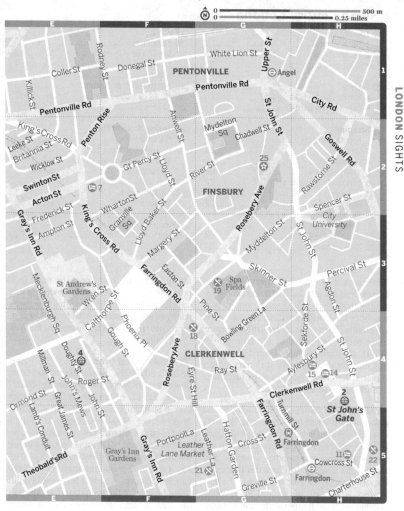

present day. The rear garden is also organised by era, mirroring the museum's exploration of domesticity through the centuries. There's also a very impressive walled herb garden, featuring 170 different plants.

⭐**St John's Gate**   HISTORIC BUILDING
(Map p106; www.museumstjohn.org.uk; St John's Lane, EC1M; tour suggested donation £5; ⊙10am-5pm Mon-Sat year-round, 10am-5pm Sun July-Aug, tours 11am & 2.30pm Tue, Fri & Sat; ⊜Farringdon) **FREE** This remarkable Tudor gate dates to 1504. During the 12th century, the Knights Hospitaller (a Christian and military order

with a focus on providing care to the sick) established a priory here. Inside is a small museum that covers the history of the order (including rare examples of the knights' armour), as well as its 19th-century revival in Britain as the secular Order of St John and the foundation of St John Ambulance.

◉ The East End & Docklands

A huge area, the East End and Docklands are not rich in sights, but a dramatic new focus has emerged in the Olympic Park, while new Overground lines make transport

North Central London

a breeze. The Docklands' Canary Wharf and Isle of Dogs are an island of tower blocks, rivalling those of the City itself. London's port was once the world's greatest, the hub of the enormous global trade of the British Empire. Since being pummelled by the Luftwaffe in WWII, its fortunes have been topsy-turvy, but massive development of Canary Wharf replaced its crusty seadogs with battalions of dark-suited office workers.

★ **Museum of London Docklands** MUSEUM (www.museumoflondon.org.uk/docklands; West India Quay, E14; ⊙10am-6pm; 🚇DLR West India Quay) FREE Housed in an 1802 warehouse, this educational museum combines artefacts and multimedia displays to chart the history of the city through its river and docks. The best strategy is to begin on the 3rd floor, where displays cover the Roman settlement of Londinium, and work your way down through the ages. Perhaps the most illuminating and certainly the most disturbing gallery is London, Sugar and Slavery, which examines the capital's role in the transatlantic slave trade.

★ **Queen Elizabeth Olympic Park** PARK (www.queenelizabetholympicpark.co.uk; E20; 🚇Stratford) The glittering centrepiece of London's 2012 Olympic Games, this vast 227-hectare expanse includes the main Olympic venues as well as playgrounds, walking and cycling trails, gardens and a diverse mix of wetland, woodland, meadow and other wildlife habitats as an environmentally

fertile legacy for the future. The main focal point is the **stadium** (www.london-stadium.com; tours adult/child £19/11), with a Games capacity of 80,000, scaled back to 54,000 seats for its new role as the home ground for West Ham United FC.

★ **ArcelorMittal Orbit** TOWER (📞0333 800 8099; www.arcelormittalorbit.com; Queen Elizabeth Olympic Park, E20; adult/child £12/7, with slide £15/10; ⊙10am-6pm Apr-Sep, to 5pm Oct-Mar; 🚇Stratford) Love it or loathe it, Turner Prize–winner Anish Kapoor's 115m-high, twisted-steel sculpture towers strikingly over the southern end of Olympic Park. In essence it's an artwork, but at the 80m mark it also offers a stunning panorama from its mirrored viewing platform, which is accessed by a lift from the base of the sculpture (the tallest in the UK). A dramatic tunnel slide running down the tower is the world's highest and longest, coiling 178m down to ground level.

House Mill HISTORIC BUILDING (www.housemill.org.uk; Three Mill Lane, E3; adult/child £3/free; ⊙11am-4pm Sun May-Oct, 1st Sun only Mar, Apr & Dec; 🚇Bromley-by-Bow) One of two remaining mills from a trio that once stood on this small island in the River Lea, House Mill (1776) operated as a sluice tidal mill, grinding grain for a nearby distillery until 1941. Tours, which run according to demand and last about 45 minutes, take visitors to all four floors of the mill and offer a fascinating look at traditional East End industry.

★ **Viktor Wynd Museum of Curiosities, Fine Art & Natural History** MUSEUM
(www.thelasttuesdaysociety.org; 11 Mare St, E8; admission £5; ⊘11am-10pm Wed-Sun; ⊜Bethnal Green) Museum? Art project? Cocktail bar? This is not a venue that's easily classifiable. Inspired by Victorian-era cabinets of curiosities (*wunderkabinnet*), Wynd's wilfully eccentric collection includes stuffed birds, pickled genitals, two-headed lambs, shrunken heads, a key to the Garden of Eden, dodo bones, celebrity excrement, ancient Chinese dildos and toys from McDonald's Happy Meals. A self-confessed 'incoherent vision of the world displayed through wonder', make of it what you will. Or stop by for a cocktail (£8) at the tiny bar.

◎ Greenwich

Greenwich (*gren*-itch) straddles the hemispheres and the ages, retaining its own sense of identity based on historic associations with the sea and science and an extraordinary cluster of buildings that have earned 'Maritime Greenwich' a Unesco World Heritage listing.

★ **Old Royal Naval College** HISTORIC BUILDING
(www.ornc.org; 2 Cutty Sark Gardens, SE10; ⊘grounds 8am-6pm, to 11pm in summer; ⊠DLR Cutty Sark) **FREE** Designed by Christopher Wren, the Old Royal Naval College is a magnificent example of monumental classical architecture. Parts are now used by the University of Greenwich and Trinity College of Music, but you can still visit the chapel and the extraordinary Painted Hall, which took artist Sir James Thornhill 19 years to complete. Hour-long, yeomen-led tours (£6) leave at noon daily, taking in areas not otherwise open to the public. Free 45-minute tours take place at least four times daily.

★ **National Maritime Museum** MUSEUM
(www.rmg.co.uk/national-maritime-museum; Romney Rd, SE10; ⊘10am-5pm; ⊠DLR Cutty Sark) **FREE** Narrating the long, briny and eventful history of seafaring Britain, this excellent museum's exhibits are arranged thematically, with highlights including *Miss Britain III* (the first boat to top 100mph on open water) from 1933, the 19m-long golden state barge built in 1732 for Frederick, Prince of Wales, the huge ship's propeller and the colourful figureheads installed on the ground floor. Families will love these, as well as the ship simulator and the 'All Hands' children's gallery on the 2nd floor.

★ **Royal Observatory** HISTORIC BUILDING
(www.rmg.co.uk; Greenwich Park, Blackheath Ave, SE10; adult/child £9.50/5, with Cutty Sark £18.50/8.50; ⊘10am-5pm Sep-Jun, to 6pm Jul & Aug; ⊠DLR Cutty Sark, ⊠DLR Greenwich, ⊠Greenwich) Rising south of Queen's House, idyllic Greenwich Park (www.royalparks.org.uk; King George St, SE10; ⊘6am-6pm winter, to 8pm spring & autumn, to 9pm summer; ⊠DLR Cutty Sark, ⊠Greenwich or Maze Hill) climbs up the hill, affording stunning views of London from the Royal Observatory, which Charles II had built in 1675 to help solve the riddle of longitude. To the north is lovely Flamsteed House and the Meridian Courtyard, where you can stand with your feet straddling the western and eastern hemispheres; admission is by ticket. The southern half contains the highly informative and free Weller Astronomy Galleries and the Peter Harrison Planetarium (☎020-8312 6608; www.rmg.co.uk/whats-on/planetarium-shows; adult/child £7.50/5.50).

Queen's House HISTORIC BUILDING
(www.rmg.co.uk/queens-house; Romney Rd, SE10; ⊘10am-5pm; ⊠DLR Cutty Sark) **FREE** The first Palladian building by architect Inigo Jones after he returned from Italy is as enticing for its form as for its art collection. The Great Hall is a lovely cube shape with an elaborately

EMIRATES AIR LINE CABLE CAR

Capable of ferrying 2400 people per hour across the Thames in either direction, the cable car run by Emirates Air Line (www.emiratesairline.co.uk; 27 Western Gateway, E16; one-way adult/child £4.50/2.30, with Oyster Card or Travelcard £3.40/1.70; ⊘7am-9pm Mon-Fri, 8am-9pm Sat, 9am-9pm Sun, closes 8pm Oct-Mar; ⊠DLR Royal Victoria, ⊜North Greenwich) makes quick work of the journey from the Greenwich Peninsula to the Royal Docks. Although it's mostly patronised by tourists for the views over the river – and the views are ace – it's also listed on the London Underground map as part of the transport network. Oyster Card and Travelcard holders nab discounts for journeys, which are bike-friendly, too.

The River Thames

A FLOATING TOUR

London's history has always been determined by the Thames. The city was founded as a Roman port nearly 2000 years ago and over the centuries since then many of the capital's landmarks have lined the river's banks. A boat trip is a great way to experience the attractions.

There are piers dotted along both banks at regular intervals where you can hop on and hop off the regular services to visit places of interest. The best place to board is Westminster Pier, from where boats head downstream, taking you from the City of Westminster, the seat of government, to the original City of London, now the financial district and dominated by a growing band of skyscrapers. Across the river, the once shabby and neglected South Bank now bristles with as many top attractions as its northern counterpart, including the slender Shard.

In our illustration we've concentrated on the top highlights you'll enjoy from a waterborne

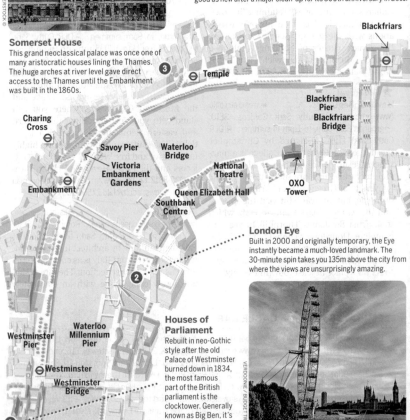

KIEV.VICTOR / SHUTTERSTOCK ©

St Paul's Cathedral
Though there's been a church here since AD 604, the current building rose from the ashes of the 1666 Great Fire and is architect Christopher Wren's masterpiece. Famous for surviving the Blitz intact and for the wedding of Charles and Diana, it's looking as good as new after a major clean-up for its 300th anniversary in 2011.

Blackfriars

Somerset House
This grand neoclassical palace was once one of many aristocratic houses lining the Thames. The huge arches at river level gave direct access to the Thames until the Embankment was built in the 1860s.

Temple

Blackfriars Pier
Blackfriars Bridge

Charing Cross

Savoy Pier
Waterloo Bridge

Victoria Embankment Gardens

National Theatre

OXO Tower

Embankment

Queen Elizabeth Hall
Southbank Centre

London Eye
Built in 2000 and originally temporary, the Eye instantly became a much-loved landmark. The 30-minute spin takes you 135m above the city from where the views are unsurprisingly amazing.

Houses of Parliament
Rebuilt in neo-Gothic style after the old Palace of Westminster burned down in 1834, the most famous part of the British parliament is the clocktower. Generally known as Big Ben, it's named after Benjamin Hall who oversaw its construction.

Westminster Pier
Waterloo Millennium Pier

Westminster
Westminster Bridge

VERDOONE / BUDGET TRAVEL ©

vessel. These are, from west to east, the **Houses of Parliament** ❶, the **London Eye** ❷, **Somerset House** ❸, **St Paul's Cathedral** ❹, **Tate Modern** ❺, **Shakespeare's Globe** ❻, the **Tower of London** ❼ and **Tower Bridge** ❽.

Apart from covering this central section of the river, boats can also be taken upstream as far as Kew Gardens and Hampton Court Palace, and downstream to Greenwich and the Thames Barrier.

BOAT HOPPING

Thames Clippers hop-on/hop-off services are aimed at commuters but are equally useful for visitors, operating every 15 minutes on a loop from piers at Embankment, Waterloo, Blackfriars, Bankside, London Bridge and the Tower. Other services also go from Westminster. Oyster cardholders get a discount off the boat ticket price.

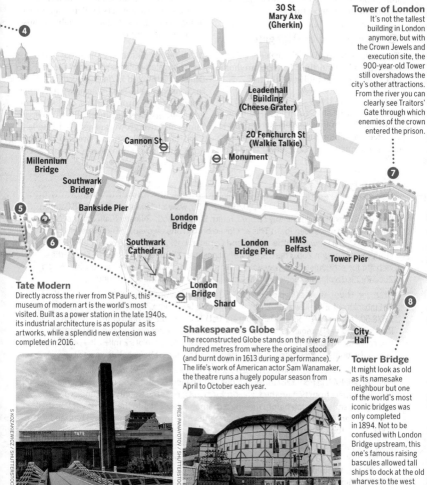

30 St Mary Axe (Gherkin)

Leadenhall Building (Cheese Grater)

20 Fenchurch St (Walkie Talkie)

Cannon St

Monument

Millennium Bridge

Southwark Bridge

Bankside Pier

London Bridge

Southwark Cathedral

London Bridge

Shard

London Bridge Pier

HMS Belfast

Tower Pier

City Hall

Tower of London
It's not the tallest building in London anymore, but with the Crown Jewels and execution site, the 900-year-old Tower still overshadows the city's other attractions. From the river you can clearly see Traitors' Gate through which enemies of the crown entered the prison.

Tate Modern
Directly across the river from St Paul's, this museum of modern art is the world's most visited. Built as a power station in the late 1940s, its industrial architecture is as popular as its artworks, while a splendid new extension was completed in 2016.

Shakespeare's Globe
The reconstructed Globe stands on the river a few hundred metres from where the original stood (and burnt down in 1613 during a performance). The life's work of American actor Sam Wanamaker, the theatre runs a hugely popular season from April to October each year.

Tower Bridge
It might look as old as its namesake neighbour but one of the world's most iconic bridges was only completed in 1894. Not to be confused with London Bridge upstream, this one's famous raising bascules allowed tall ships to dock at the old wharves to the west and are still lifted up to 1000 times a year.

S. KOZANIEWICZ / SHUTTERSTOCK ©

PRES PANAYOTOV / SHUTTERSTOCK ©

tiled floor. Climb the beautiful helix-shaped Tulip Stairs up to the 1st floor, where there's a rich collection of paintings and portraits with a sea or seafaring theme from the National Maritime Museum's collection.

★**Cutty Sark**   MUSEUM
(☏020-8312 6608; www.rmg.co.uk/cuttysark; King William Walk, SE10; adult/child £13.50/7, with Royal Observatory £18.50/8.50; ◷10am-5pm Sep-Jun, to 6pm Jul & Aug; ⟐DLR Cutty Sark) This Greenwich landmark, the last of the great clipper ships to sail between China and England in the 19th century, saw £25 million of extensive renovations largely precipitated by a disastrous fire in 2007. The exhibition in the ship's hold tells its story as a tea clipper at the end of the 19th century.

◉ Hampstead & Highgate

These quaint and well-heeled villages, perched on hills north of London, are home to a litany of A- and B-list celebrities.

★**Hampstead Heath**   PARK
(⊖Hampstead Heath) Sprawling Hampstead Heath, with its rolling woodlands and meadows, feels a million miles away – despite being approximately 4 miles – from the City of

London. Covering 320 hectares, most of it woods, hills and meadows, it's home to about 180 bird species, 23 species of butterflies, grass snakes, bats and a rich array of flora.

★**Kenwood**   HISTORIC BUILDING
(EH; www.english-heritage.org.uk; Hampstead Lane, NW3; ◷10am-5pm; ▣210) **FREE** This magnificent neoclassical mansion stands at the northern end of Hampstead Heath in a glorious sweep of landscaped gardens leading down to a picturesque lake. The 17th-century house was substantially remodelled in the 1760s and rescued from developers by Edward Cecil Guinness, 1st Earl of Iveagh, who donated it and the wonderful collection of art it contains to the nation in 1927. Among its treasures are paintings by such greats as Rembrandt (one of his many self-portraits), Constable, Gainsborough and Vermeer.

★**Highgate Cemetery**   CEMETERY
(www.highgatecemetery.org; Swain's Lane, N6; East Cemetery adult/child £4/free; ◷10am-5pm Mon-Fri, 11am-5pm Sat & Sun; ⊖Archway) A Gothic wonderland of shrouded urns, obelisks, broken columns, sleeping angels, Egyptian-style tombs and overgrown graves, Highgate is a Victorian Valhalla spread over 20 wonderfully wild and atmospheric hectares. On

---

TRIPS ON THE THAMES

London Waterbus Company (☏020-7482 2550; www.londonwaterbus.co.uk; 58 Camden Lock Pl, NW1; adult/child one-way £8.50/7, return £12.50/10.50; ◷hourly 10am-5pm Apr-Sep; ⊖Warwick Ave or Camden Town) This enclosed barge runs enjoyable 50-minute trips on Regent's Canal between Little Venice and Camden Lock, passing by Regent's Park and stopping at London Zoo. There are fewer departures outside high season – check the website for schedules. One-way tickets (adult/child £25/18), including entry to London Zoo, are also available for passengers to disembark within the zoo grounds.

Thames River Boats (Map p72; ☏020-7930 2062; www.wpsa.co.uk; Westminster Pier, Victoria Embankment, SW1; Kew adult/child one-way £13/6.50, return £20/10, Hampton Court one-way £17/8.50, return £25/12.50; ◷10am-4pm Apr-Oct) These boats go upriver from Westminster Pier to the Royal Botanic Gardens at Kew (1½ hours, four per day) and on to Hampton Court Palace (another 1½ hours, 11am sailing only), a distance of 22 miles. It's possible to get off the boats at Richmond, but it depends on the tides; check before you sail.

London Duck Tours (Map p92; ☏020-7928 3132; www.londonducktours.co.uk; County Hall, SE1; adult/child from £26/18; ⊖Waterloo) Amphibious craft based on D-Day landing vehicles depart from behind the **London Eye** (p90) near the County Hall and cruise the streets of central London before making a dramatic descent into the Thames at Vauxhall. There's a variety of tours, from the classic sightseeing tour to a James Bond tour and a D Day Duck tour, as well as private tours.

City Cruises (Map p72; ☏020-7740 0400; www.citycruises.com; single/return from £12.50/16.50, day pass £16.65) Ferry service departing every 30 minutes between Westminster, the London Eye, Bankside, Tower and Greenwich piers, with circular cruises (£11.70) going from Tower and Bankside.

the eastern side, you can pay your respects to the graves of Karl Marx and Mary Ann Evans (better known as novelist George Eliot). The real highlight, however, is the overgrown **West Cemetery**, which can only be visited on a **guided tour** (adult/child £12/6; ⊘1.45pm Mon-Fri, every 30min 11am-3pm Sat & Sun Nov-Mar, to 4pm Apr-Oct); bookings are essential for weekday tours.

⊙ Outside Central London

★**Kew Gardens**   GARDENS
(www.kew.org; Kew Rd; adult/child £15/3.50; ⊘10am-6.30pm Apr-Aug, closes earlier Sep-Mar; 🚇Kew Pier, 🚉Kew Bridge, ⊖Kew Gardens) In 1759 botanists began rummaging around the world for specimens to plant in the 3-hectare Royal Botanic Gardens at Kew. They never stopped collecting, and the gardens, which have bloomed to 120 hectares, provide the most comprehensive botanical collection on earth (including the world's largest collection of orchids). A Unesco World Heritage Site, the gardens can easily devour a day's exploration; for those pressed for time, the **Kew Explorer** (adult/child £5/2) hop-on/hop-off road train takes in the main sights.

Don't worry if you don't know your golden slipper orchid from your fengoky or your quiver tree from your alang-alang; a visit to Kew is a journey of discovery for everyone. Highlights include the enormous early **Victorian Palm House**, a hothouse of metal and curved sheets of glass; the impressive **Princess of Wales Conservatory**; the red-brick, 1631 **Kew Palace** (www.hrp.org.uk/kewpalace; with admission to Kew Gardens; ⊘10.30am-5.30pm Apr-Sep), formerly King George III's country retreat; the celebrated **Chinese Pagoda** designed by William Chambers in 1762 (closed for restoration until 2018); the **Temperate House**, the world's largest ornamental glasshouse (closed for restoration until 2018); and the very enjoyable **Rhizotron & Xstrata Treetop Walkway**, where you can survey the tree canopy from 18m up in the air. A lattice fashioned from thousands of pieces of aluminium illuminated with hundreds of LED lights, the 17m-high **Hive** mimics activity within a real beehive (it's on show till late 2017). Check the website for a full list of activities at Kew from free one-hour walking tours (daily), photography walks, theatre performances, outside cinema as well as a host of seasonal events and things to do.

WORTH A TRIP

ABBEY ROAD STUDIOS
Beatles aficionados can't possibly visit London without making a pilgrimage to the famous **Abbey Road Studios** (www.abbeyroad.com; 3 Abbey Rd, NW8; ⊖St John's Wood) in St John's Wood. The recording studios themselves are off-limits, so you'll have to content yourself with examining the decades of fans' graffiti on the fence outside. Stop-start local traffic is long accustomed to groups of tourists lining up on the zebra crossing to re-enact the cover of the fab four's 1969 masterpiece *Abbey Road*. In 2010 the crossing was rewarded with Grade II heritage status.

Kew Gardens are easily reached by tube, but you might prefer to take a cruise on a riverboat from the **Westminster Passenger Services Association** (Map p72; ⊘020-7930 2062; www.wpsa.co.uk; return to Hampton Court adult/child £25/12.50; ⊖Westminster), which runs several daily boats from April to October, departing from Westminster Pier.

★**Hampton Court Palace**   PALACE
(www.hrp.org.uk/hamptoncourtpalace; adult/child/family £19/9.50/47; ⊘10am-6pm Apr-Oct, to 4.30pm Nov-Mar; 🚇Hampton Court Palace, 🚉Hampton Court) Built by Cardinal Thomas Wolsey in 1514 but coaxed from him by Henry VIII just before Wolsey (as chancellor) fell from favour, Hampton Court Palace is England's largest and grandest Tudor structure. It was already one of Europe's most sophisticated palaces when, in the 17th century, Christopher Wren designed an extension. The result is a beautiful blend of Tudor and 'restrained baroque' architecture. You could easily spend a day exploring the palace and its 24 hectares of riverside gardens, including a 300-year-old **maze** (adult/child/family £4.40/2.80/13.20; ⊘10am-5.15pm Apr-Oct, to 3.45pm Nov-Mar).

Take a themed tour led by costumed historians or, if you're in a rush, visit the highlights: **Henry VIII's State Apartments**, including the **Great Hall** with its spectacular hammer-beamed roof; the **Tudor Kitchens**, staffed by 'servants'; the **Wolsey Closet**; the **Chapel Royal**; **William III's & Mary II's Apartments**, the **King's Staircase** and the **Chocolate Kitchens**; Mantegna's **The Triumphs of Caesar**; the restored and recently opened **Cumberland Art Gallery** off Clock

Court; and the magnificent gardens, including the **Kitchen Garden** – and don't miss getting lost in the maze. The **Magic Garden** is a new interactive garden attraction for children and families. Also keep an eye out for the **Real Tennis Court**, dating from the 1620s. Do not overlook exploring the palace's magnificent riverside **gardens**; on a sunny day it reveals London at its very finest and most beautiful. Check the schedule for spectacular shows and **events**, including Tudor jousting, falconry displays, ghost hunts (for children), garden adventures, family trails and more. In summer, fun 15- to 20-minute shire-horse-drawn **charabanc tours** (adult/child £6/3) depart from the East Front Garden between 11am and 5pm.

Ask one of the red-tunic-garbed warders for anecdotes and information. The excellent **audio guides** can be picked up just off Base Court and then dropped off in the bin as you exit the palace to the gardens.

Hampton Court is 13 miles southwest of central London and is easily reached by train from Waterloo. Alternatively, the riverboats that head from Westminster to Kew continue here (adult/child £17/8.50, three hours).

See p112 for more information.

Richmond Park   PARK

(☉ 7am-dusk; ☒ Richmond) At almost 1000 hectares (the largest urban parkland in Europe), this park offers everything from formal gardens and ancient oaks to unsurpassed views of central London 12 miles away. It's easy to flee the several roads slicing up the rambling wilderness, making the park perfect for a quiet walk or a picnic with the kids, even in summer when Richmond's riverside heaves. Coming from Richmond, it's easiest to enter via Richmond Gate or from Petersham Rd.

Strawberry Hill   HISTORIC BUILDING

(www.strawberryhillhouse.org.uk; 268 Waldegrave Rd, TW1; adult/child £12/free; ☉ house 1.40-5.30pm Mon-Wed, noon-5.30pm Sat & Sun Mar-Oct, garden 10am-6pm daily; ☒ Strawberry Hill, ☒ Richmond Station, then bus R68) With its snow-white walls and Gothic turrets, this fantastical and totally restored 18th-century creation in Twickenham is the work of art historian, author and politician Horace Walpole. Studded with elaborate stained glass, the building reaches its astonishing apogee in the gallery, with its magnificent papier-mâché ceiling. For the full magic, join a twilight tour (£20). Last admission to the house is 4pm.

Wimbledon Lawn
Tennis Museum   MUSEUM

(☎ 020-8946 6131; www.wimbledon.com/museum; Gate 4, Church Rd, SW19; adult/child £13/8, museum & tour £24/15; ☉ 10am-5.30pm, last admission 5pm; ☒ Wimbledon, then bus 93, ☒ Wimbledon) This ace museum details the history of tennis – from its French precursor *jeu de paume* (which employed the open hand) to the supersonic serves of today's champions. It's a state-of-the-art presentation, with plenty of video clips and a projection of John McEnroe in the dressing room at Wimbledon, but the highlight is the chance to see Centre Court from the **360-degree viewing box**. During the championships in June/July, only those with tickets to the tournament can access the museum.

☞ Tours

From erudite to eccentric, tours on offer to see the sights are legion in London. Bus tours, although not particularly cool, are good for those who are short on time. Those with special interests – Jewish London, bird watching, pop music – might consider hiring their own guide.

Original Tour   BUS

(www.theoriginaltour.com; adult/child £30/15; ☉ 8.30am-8.30pm) A 24-hour hop-on, hop-off bus service with a river cruise thrown in, as well as three themed walks: Changing of the Guard, Rock 'n' Roll and Jack the Ripper. Buses run every five to 20 minutes; you can buy tickets on the bus or online. There's also a 48-hour ticket available (adult/child £40/19), with an extended river cruise.

Big Bus Tours   BUS

(www.bigbustours.com; adult/child £26/12.50; ☉ every 20min 8.30am-6pm Apr-Sep, to 5pm Oct & Mar, to 4.30pm Nov-Feb) Informative commentaries in 12 languages. The ticket includes a free river cruise with City Cruises and three thematic walking tours (Royal London, film locations, mysteries). Good online booking discounts available.

London Mystery Walks   WALKING

(☎ 07957 388280; www.tourguides.org.uk; adult/child/family £10/9/20) Tour Jack the Ripper's old haunts at 7pm on Monday, Wednesday, Friday and Sunday. London chocolate tours too (£39) on Sunday at 12.30pm. You must book in advance.

London Beatles Walks   WALKING

(☎ 07958 706329; www.beatlesinlondon.com; adult/child £10/free) Public and private tours following in the footsteps of the fab four. Most tours are just over two hours.

London Bicycle Tour CYCLING
(Map p92; ☎020-7928 6838; www.londonbicycle.com; 1 Gabriel's Wharf, 56 Upper Ground, SE1; tour incl bike from £23.95, bike hire per day £20; ⊕Southwark, Waterloo or Blackfriars) Three-hour tours begin in the South Bank and take in London's highlights on both sides of the river; a night ride is also available. You can also hire traditional or speciality bikes, such as tandems and folding bikes, by the hour or day.

Activities

London Aquatics Centre SWIMMING
(www.londonaquaticscentre.org; Queen Elizabeth Olympic Park, E20; adult/child £4.95/2.50; ⊙6am-10.30pm; ⊕Stratford) The sweeping lines and wave-like movement of Zaha Hadid's award-winning Aquatics Centre make it the architectural highlight of Olympic Park (p108). Bathed in natural light, the 50m competition pool beneath the huge undulating roof (which sits on just three supports) is an extraordinary place to swim. There's also a second 50m pool, a diving area, gym, creche and cafe.

Lee Valley VeloPark CYCLING
(☎0300 0030 610; www.visitleevalley.org.uk/velopark; Abercrombie Rd, E20; 1hr taster adult/child £40/30, pay & ride weekend/weekday £5/4, bike & helmet hire from £8; ⊙9am-10pm; ⊕Hackney Wick) An architectural highlight of Olympic Park (p108) is the cutting-edge velodrome that is open to the public – either to wander through and watch the pros tear around the steep-sloped circuit, or to have a go yourself. Both the velodrome and the attached BMX park offer taster sessions. Mountain bikers and road cyclists can attack the tracks on a pay-and-ride basis.

Up at the O2 ADVENTURE SPORTS
(www.theo2.co.uk/upattheo2; O2, Greenwich Peninsula, SE10; weekdays/weekends from £28/35; ⊙hours vary; ⊕North Greenwich) London isn't exactly your thrill-seeking destination, but this ascent of the O2 dome is not for the faint-hearted. Equipped with climbing suit and harness, you'll scale the famous white dome to reach a viewing platform perched 52m above the Thames with sweeping views of Canary Wharf, the river, Greenwich and beyond. Hours vary depending on the season (sunset climbs also available).

★ Festivals & Events

Chinese New Year CULTURAL
(⊙late Jan or early Feb) Chinese New Year sees Chinatown snap, crackle and pop with fireworks, a colourful street parade and eating aplenty.

University Boat Race ROWING
(www.theboatrace.org; ⊙late Mar) A posh-boy grudge match held annually since 1829 between the rowing crews of Oxford and Cambridge universities.

Virgin Money London Marathon MARATHON
(www.virginmoneylondonmarathon.com; ⊙late Apr) Up to half a million spectators watch the whippet-thin champions and bizarrely clad amateurs take to the streets.

Chelsea Flower Show HORTICULTURE
(www.rhs.org.uk/chelsea; Royal Hospital Chelsea; admission from £23; ⊙May) Arguably the world's most renowned horticultural show attracts green fingers from near and far.

Trooping the Colour PARADE
(⊙Jun) Celebrating the Queen's official birthday, this ceremonial procession of troops, marching along the Mall for their monarch's inspection, is a pageantry overload.

Field Day MUSIC
(www.fielddayfestivals.com; Victoria Park, Grove Rd, E3; ⊙Jun; ⊕Hackney Wick) The annual Field Day music festival has been running in Victoria Park (www.towerhamlets.gov.uk/victoriapark; Grove Rd, E3; ⊙7am-dusk; ⊕Hackney Wick) since 2007, with performances in recent years from PJ Harvey, Air and James Blake.

Royal Academy Summer Exhibition ART
(www.royalacademy.org.uk; adult/child £9.50/5; ⊙mid-Jun–mid-Aug) This is an annual showcase of works submitted by artists from all over Britain, mercifully distilled to 1200 or so pieces.

OUTDOOR CITY SWIMMING

Built in the 1930s but abandoned by the '80s, the London Fields Lido (☎020-7254 9038; www.better.org.uk/leisure/london-fields-lido; London Fields Westside, E8; adult/child £4.80/2.85; ⊙6.30am-9pm; ⊕Hackney Central) heated 50m Olympic-size outdoor pool gets packed with swimmers and sunbathers during summer.

Hampton Court Palace

A DAY AT THE PALACE

With so much to explore and seemingly infinite gardens, it can be tricky knowing where to begin. It helps to understand how the palace has grown over the centuries and how successive royal occupants embellished Hampton Court to suit their purposes and to reflect the style of the time.

As soon as he had his royal hands upon the palace from Cardinal Thomas Wolsey,

Henry VIII began expanding the **Tudor architecture** ❶, adding the **Great Hall** ❷, the exquisite **Chapel Royal** ❸, the opulent Great Watching Chamber and the gigantic **kitchens** ❹. By 1540 it had become one of the grandest and most sophisticated palaces in Europe. James I kept things ticking over, while Charles I added a new tennis court and did some serious art-collecting, including pieces that can be seen in the recently opened **Cumberland Art Gallery** ❺.

Tudor Kitchens

These vast kitchens were the engine room of the palace. With a staff of 200 people, there were six spit-rack-equipped fireplaces, with roast meat always on the menu (to the tune of 8200 sheep and 1240 oxen per year).

VISITBRITAIN / GETTY IMAGES ©

❼ The Maze

Around 150m north of the main bulding
Created from hornbeam and yew and planted in around 1700, the maze covers a third of an acre within the famous palace gardens. A must-see conclusion to Hampton Court, the maze takes the average visitor about 20 minutes to reach the centre.

Tudor Architecture

Dating to 1515, the heart of the palace serves as one of the finest examples of Tudor architecture in the nation. Cardinal Thomas Wolsey was responsible for transforming what was originally a grand medieval manor house into a stunning Tudor palace.

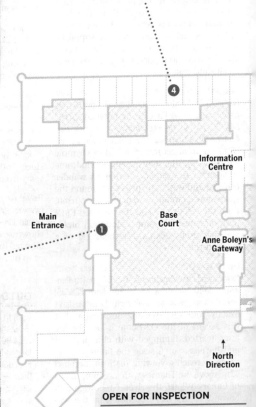

Information Centre

Main Entrance

Base Court

Anne Boleyn's Gateway

↑ North Direction

KIEVVICTOR / SHUTTERSTOCK ©

OPEN FOR INSPECTION

The palace was opened to the public by Queen Victoria in 1838.

After the Civil War, puritanical Oliver Cromwell warmed to his own regal proclivities, spending weekends in the comfort of the former Queen's bedroom and selling off Charles I's art collection. In the late 17th century, William and Mary employed Sir Christopher Wren for baroque extensions, chiefly the William III Apartments, reached by the **King's Staircase** ⑥. William III also commissioned the world-famous **maze** ⑦.

TOP TIPS

» Ask one of the red-tunic-garbed warders for anecdotes and information.

» Tag along with a themed tour led by costumed historians or hop on a shire horse-drawn charabanc tour of the east garden in summer.

» Grab one of the audio tours from the Information Centre.

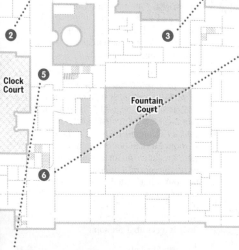

The Great Hall
This grand dining hall is the defining room of the palace, displaying what is considered England's finest hammer-beam roof, 16th-century Flemish tapestries telling the story of Abraham, and some exquisite stained-glass windows.

Chapel Royal
The blue-and-gold vaulted ceiling was originally intended for Christ Church, Oxford, but was installed here instead; the 18th-century oak reredos was carved by Grinling Gibbons. Books on display include a 1611 1st edition of the King James Bible, printed by Robert Barker.

The King's Staircase
One of five rooms at the palace painted by Antonio Verrio and a suitably bombastic prelude to the King's Apartments, the overblown King's Staircase adulates William III by elevating him above a cohort of Roman emperors.

Cumberland Art Gallery
The former Cumberland Suite, designed by William Kent, has been restored to accommodate a choice selection of some of the finest works from the Royal Collection.

WHY I LOVE LONDON

By Steve Fallon, Writer

Like most Londoners, I revel in all our familiar landmarks – Big Ben, Tower Bridge, the murky Thames, the London Eye. I still thank the former government that made some of the greatest museums and art galleries in the world free to one and all. The choice of restaurants, bars and clubs is legion, and what's not to love about a city with more lush parkland than any other world capital? But the one thing that sets my adopted city apart from any other is its amazing tolerance. 'As long as you don't scare the horses, mate, you'll be all right here,' I was told when I arrived here more than 20 years ago. Guess what...it still hasn't happened.

Meltdown Festival   MUSIC
(www.southbankcentre.co.uk; ⊙ late Jun) The Southbank Centre hands over the curatorial reigns to a legend of contemporary music (Morrissey, Patti Smith or David Byrne) to pull together a full program of concerts, talks and films.

**Wimbledon Lawn Tennis
Championships**   SPORTS
(www.wimbledon.com; ⊙ late Jun; ⊖ Wimbledon) The world's most splendid tennis event takes place in late June.

Wireless   MUSIC
(www.wirelessfestival.co.uk; Finsbury Park, N4; ⊙ Jul) This popular rock and pop festival is held over three days in July every year.

Pride   GAY & LESBIAN
(www.prideinlondon.org; ⊙ late Jun or early Jul) The big event on the gay and lesbian calendar, a technicolour street parade heads through the West End, culminating in a concert in Trafalgar Sq.

Lovebox   MUSIC
(www.loveboxfestival.com; Victoria Park, E9; ⊙ mid-Jul) London's contribution to the summer music-festival circuit, held in Victoria Park.

Notting Hill Carnival   CARNIVAL
(www.thenottinghillcarnival.com; ⊙ Aug) Every year, for three days during the last weekend of August, Notting Hill echoes to the calypso, ska, reggae and soca sounds of the Notting Hill Carnival. Launched in 1964 by the local Afro-Caribbean community, keen to celebrate its culture and traditions, it has grown to become Europe's largest street festival (up to one million people) and a highlight of London's calendar.

🛏 Sleeping

Hanging your hat (and anything else you care to remove) in London can be painfully expensive, and you'll almost always need to book your room well in advance. Decent, central hostels are easy enough to find and also offer reasonably priced double rooms. Bed and breakfasts are a dependable and inexpensive, if rather simple, option. Hotels range from cheap, no-frills chains through boutique choices to luxury five-star historic hotels.

🛏 West End

Like in Monopoly, land on a Mayfair hotel and you may have to sell your house, or at least remortgage. This is the heart of the action, and a couple of hostels cater for would be Soho hipsters of more modest means.

YHA London Oxford Street   HOSTEL £
(Map p78; 🕿 020-7734 1618; www.yha.org.uk; 14 Noel St, W1; dm/tw from £18/46; @ 🛜; ⊖ Oxford Circus) The most central of London's eight YHA hostels is also one of the most intimate with just 104 beds, and excellent shared facilities, including the fuchsia kitchen and the bright, funky lounge. Dormitories have three and four beds and there are doubles and twins. The in-house shop sells coffee and beer. Wi-fi (common areas) is free. Free daily walking tours too.

Morgan Hotel   B&B ££
(Map p78; 🕿 020-7636 3735; www.morganhotel. co.uk; 24 Bloomsbury St, WC1; s/d/tr incl breakfast £120/145/165, ste from £175; ✳@🛜; ⊖ Tottenham Court Rd) In a delightful row of 18th-century Georgian houses, the family-owned 17-room Morgan offers friendliness, fine service, breakfast fit for a king, and excellent value for central London. Room decor may be somewhat dated, but cleanliness is a strong point. Larger suites (single/double/triple £175/205/250, no air-con) are worth the extra outlay. There's no lift, and the top floor is a clamber for some.

Jesmond Hotel   B&B ££
(Map p106; 🕿 020-7636 3199; www.jesmondhotel. org.uk; 63 Gower St, WC1; s/d/tr/q incl breakfast from £70/90/120/150; @🛜; ⊖ Goodge St) The

rooms – cheapest with shared bathroom – at this popular, 15-room family-run Georgian hotel in Bloomsbury are basic but clean and cheerful, there's a small, pretty garden and the price tag is very attractive indeed. There's also laundry service, free wi-fi and good breakfasts for kicking off your London day. Location is highly central.

★ **Beaumont** HOTEL £££
(Map p101; ☑ 020-7499 1001; www.thebeaumont. com; Brown Hart Gardens, W1; d/studio/ste incl breakfast from £395/625/900; ✱ ☞; ⊖ Bond St) A stylish, handsome and luxurious hotel, the 73-room Beaumont is all deco opulence. Fronted by an arresting chunk of deco-inspired stainless steel and fumed oak sculpture from Antony Gormley called *Room* (part of a £1130-per-night suite), the striking white building dates from 1926. Rooms and suites are swish and elegant, with a 1920s modernist aesthetic. Room prices include local drop-offs in the hotel's vintage Daimler.

★ **Corinthia** HOTEL £££
(Map p78; ☑ 020-7930 8181; www.corinthia. com; Whitehall Place, SW1; d/ste/penthouse £425/1380/3000; ✱ ☞ ⊠; ⊖ Embankment) With hotels from Malta to St Petersburg, the Corinthia group's crown jewel is this grand Victorian property in Whitehall. It's as smart as can be, but never overbearing and stuffy. A stay here is a delight, from perfect rooms to flawless service, tempting afternoon tea and a location that ensconces you at the very heart, but just beyond the bustle of London.

★ **Haymarket Hotel** HOTEL £££
(Map p78; ☑ 020-7470 4000; www.haymarket hotel.com; 1 Suffolk Pl, off Haymarket, SW1; r/ste from £336/504; ✱ ☞ ⊠; ⊖ Piccadilly Circus) With the trademark colours and lines of hoteliers and designers Tim and Kit Kemp, the Haymarket is beautiful, with hand-painted Gournay wallpaper, signature fuchsia and green designs in the 50 guest rooms, a sensational 18m pool with mood lighting, an exquisite library lounge with honesty bar, and original artwork throughout. Just love the dog silhouettes on the chairs and bar stools.

★ **Rosewood** HOTEL £££
(Map p78; ☑ 020-7781 8888; www.rosewood hotels.com/en/london; 252 High Holborn, WC1; d from £380-750, ste £1140-9000; ✱ @ ☞; ⊖ Holborn) An £85-million refurb transformed the grand Pearl Assurance building (dating from 1914) into the stunning Rosewood ho-

tel, where an artful marriage of period and modern styles can be found in its 262 rooms and 44 suites. British heritage is carefully woven throughout the bar, restaurant, deli, lobby and even the housekeepers' uniforms.

★ **Ritz** LUXURY HOTEL £££
(Map p78; ☑ 020-7493 8181; www.theritzlondon. com; 150 Piccadilly, W1; r/ste from £380/770; ✱ @ ☞; ⊖ Green Park) What can you say about a hotel that has lent its name to the English lexicon? This 136-room caravanserai has a spectacular position overlooking Green Park and is supposedly the Royal Family's home away from home (it does have a royal warrant from the Prince of Wales and is very close to the palace). All rooms have period interiors and antique furniture.

🛏 The City

It bristles with bankers during the week, but you can often net considerable bargains in the City come weekends.

London St Paul's YHA HOSTEL £
(Map p84; ☑ 020-7236 4965; www.yha.org.uk/ hostel/london-st-pauls; 36 Carter Lane, EC4; dm £17-30, d £65-79; @ ☞; ⊖ St Paul's) This 213-bed hostel is housed in the former boarding school for choir boys from St Paul's Cathedral, almost next door. Dorms have between three and 11 beds, and twins and doubles are available. There's a great lounge, licensed cafeteria (breakfast £5.25, dinner from £7 to £10) but no kitchen – and lots and lots of stairs (and no lift). Seven-night maximum stay.

Hotel Indigo Tower Hill BOUTIQUE HOTEL ££
(Map p84; ☑ 020-7265 1014; www.ihg.com; 142 Minories, EC3; r weekend/weekday from £100/260; ✱ ☞; ⊖ Aldgate) This branch of the US Inter-Continental group's boutique-hotel chain offers 46 differently styled rooms, all with four-poster beds and iPod docking stations. Larger-than-life drawings and photos of the neighbourhood won't let you forget where you are.

Andaz Liverpool Street HOTEL ££
(Map p84; ☑ 020-7961 1234; www.london.liver poolstreet.andaz.hyatt.com; 40 Liverpool St, EC2; r weekday/weekend from £180/365; ✱ ☞; ⊖ Liverpool St) This is the London flagship for Hyatt's sophisticated Andaz chain. There's no reception, just black-clad staff who check you in on iPads. The 267 rooms are cool and spacious, with interesting furnishings and lighting scheme. On top of this there are

LOCAL KNOWLEDGE

HOXTON HOTEL

In the heart of hip Shoreditch, the sleek Hoxton Hotel (Map p132; 020-7550 1000; www.hoxtonhotels.com; 81 Great Eastern St, EC2; r from £49; ❈ @ 🛜; ⊖ Old St) takes the easyJet approach to selling its rooms – book long enough ahead and you might pay just £49. The 210 renovated rooms are small but stylish, with flat-screen TVs, a desk, fridge with complimentary bottled water and milk, and breakfast (orange juice, granola, yoghurt, banana) in a bag delivered to your door.

five restaurants, two bars, a health club and a subterranean Masonic temple discovered during the hotel's refit in the '90s.

🛏 South Bank

Immediately on the south side of the Thames is a fab perch for reaching the central sights, while gauging the personality of South London.

St Christopher's Village HOSTEL £
(Map p92; 020-7939 9710; www.st-christophers. co.uk; 163 Borough High St, SE1; dm/r from £15.90/43; @ 🛜; ⊖ London Bridge) This 194-bed party-zone hostel has new bathrooms, fresh paint, pod beds with privacy curtains, reading lights, power sockets (British and European) and USB ports, and refurbished common areas. Its two bars, Belushi's and Dugout, are perennially popular. Dorms have four to 22 beds (female-only dorms available); breakfast and linen are included.

The hotel has another branch 100m up the road: St Christopher's Inn (Map p92; 020-7407 2392; www.st-christophers.co.uk; 121 Borough High St, SE1; dm/r from £13.90/50; @ 🛜; ⊖ London Bridge), which sits above a traditional pub. The dorms are smaller and look a little tired, but it's altogether quieter than at the Village.

★Citizen M BOUTIQUE HOTEL ££
(Map p92; 020-3519 1680; www.citizenm.com/london-bankside; 20 Lavington St, SE1; r £109-249; ❈ @ 🛜; ⊖ Southwark) If Citizen M had a motto, it would be 'less fuss, more comfort'. The hotel has done away with things it considers superfluous (room service, reception, bags of space) and instead gone all out on mattresses and bedding (heavenly super-

king-size beds), state-of-the-art technology (everything in the room from mood lighting to the TV is controlled through a tablet computer) and superb decor.

Shangri-La Hotel at the Shard HOTEL £££
(Map p92; 020-7234 8000; www.shangri-la. com/london/shangrila; 31 St Thomas St, SE1; d/ ste from £420/750; ❈ @ 🛜 ⊠; 🚇 London Bridge, ⊖ London Bridge) The UK's first five-star hotel south of the Thames has breathtaking views from the highest hotel (above ground level) in Western Europe, occupying levels 34 to 52 of the Shard. From the 35th-floor sky lobby to the rooms, the Shangri-La concocts a stylish blend of Chinese aesthetics, Asian hospitality and sharp modernity.

🛏 Pimlico & Belgravia

Lime Tree Hotel BOUTIQUE HOTEL ££
(Map p98; 020-7730 8191; www.limetreehotel. co.uk; 135-137 Ebury St, SW1; s £120-160, d & tw £180-210, tr £230 incl breakfast; @ 🛜; ⊖ Victoria) Family-run for 30 years, this beautiful 25-bedroom Georgian town-house hotel is all comfort, British designs and understated elegance. Rooms are individually decorated, many with open fireplaces and sash windows, but some are smaller than others, so enquire. There is a lovely back garden for late-afternoon rays (picnics encouraged on summer evenings). Rates include a hearty full-English breakfast. No lift.

B+B Belgravia B&B ££
(Map p98; 020-7259 8570; www.bb-belgravia. com; 64-66 Ebury St, SW1; d £79-209, studio £130-279; @ 🛜; ⊖ Victoria) This spiffing six-floor Georgian B&B, remodelled with contemporary flair, boasts crisp common areas and a chic lounge. The 17 rooms (some with shower, others with bath, half facing the street, half facing the garden) aren't enormous but there's a further batch of studio rooms with compact kitchens at No 82 Ebury St. A pleasant courtyard garden is out back. No lift.

★Goring HOTEL £££
(Map p72; 020-7396 9000; www.thegoring.com; Beeston Pl; r/ste from £395/825; ❈ 🛜; ⊖ Victoria) Kate Middleton spent her last night as a commoner in the Royal Suite (£8400 per night) before joining the Royal Family, propelling the Goring into an international media glare. Glistening with chandeliers, dotted with trademark fluffy sheep and overseen by highly professional staff, this family-owned hotel is a supremely grand,

albeit highly relaxed, slice of England and Englishness, with a sumptuous garden.

🛏 Knightsbridge

Named after a bridge over the River Westbourne, Knightsbridge is where you'll find some of London's best-known department stores and some top hotels.

Levin Hotel   HOTEL **£££**
(Map p98; ☏ 020-7589 6286; www.thelevinhotel.co.uk; 28 Basil St, SW3; r from £374, ste from £619 incl breakfast; ❋ @ 🛜; ⊖ Knightsbridge) The luxury 12-room Levin is a bijou boutique gem. Attention to detail (US, EU, UK and Asian sockets in every room, Nespresso coffee machines, fine Egyptian linen, underfloor heating in bathrooms, iPads on request), exquisite design and highly hospitable service create a delightful stay. The gorgeous continental buffet breakfast is complimentary. Room rates start at £274 in low season.

🛏 Chelsea & Kensington

Well-turned-out Chelsea and Kensington offer easy access to the museums, natty shopping choices and some of London's best-looking streets.

Meininger   HOSTEL **£**
(Map p98; ☏ 020-3318 1407; www.meiningerhostels.com; Baden Powell House, 65-67 Queen's Gate, SW7; dm £16-50, s/tw from £60/70; ❋ @ 🛜; ⊖ Gloucester Rd or South Kensington) Housed in the late-1950s Baden Powell House opposite the Natural History Museum, this 48-room German-run 'city hostel and hotel' has spick-and-span rooms – most are dorms of between four and 12 beds, with pod-like showers. There is also a handful of private rooms. There's good security and nice communal facilities, including a bar and a big roof terrace, plus a fantastic location.

★**Number Sixteen**   HOTEL **£££**
(Map p98; ☏ 020-7589 5232; www.firmdalehotels.com/hotels/london/number-sixteen; 16 Sumner Pl, SW7; s from £192, d £240-396; ❋ @ 🛜 ♨; ⊖ South Kensington) With uplifting splashes of colour, choice art and a sophisticated-but-fun design ethos, Number Sixteen is simply ravishing. There are 41 individually designed rooms, a cosy drawing room and a fully stocked library. And wait till you see the idyllic, long back garden set around a fountain, or sit down for breakfast in the light-filled conservatory. Great amenities for families.

Ampersand Hotel   BOUTIQUE HOTEL **£££**
(Map p98; ☏ 020-7589 5895; www.ampersandhotel.com; 10 Harrington Rd, SW7; s £170-192, d £216-360; ❋ @ 🛜; ⊖ South Kensington) It feels light, fresh and bubbly in the Ampersand, where smiling staff wear denims and waistcoats rather than impersonal dark suits. The common rooms are colourful and airy, and the stylish rooms are decorated with wallpaper designs celebrating the nearby arts and sciences of South Kensington's museums.

🛏 Earl's Court & Fulham

West London's Earl's Court is lively, cosmopolitan and so popular with travelling Antipodeans it's nicknamed Kangaroo Valley. There are no real sights, but it has inexpensive digs, an infectious holiday atmosphere and it's a short hop to the action. Further west and abutting the Thames, Fulham is the home of its famous riverside palace.

★**Barclay House**   B&B **££**
(☏ 077 6742 0943; www.barclayhouselondon.com; 21 Barclay Rd, SW6; s £110, d £135-168; @ 🛜; ⊖ Fulham Broadway) The three dapper, thoroughly modern and comfy bedrooms in this ship-shape Victorian house are a dream, from the Phillipe Starck shower rooms, walnut furniture, new double-glazed sash windows and underfloor heating to the small, thoughtful details (fumble-free coat hangers, drawers packed with sewing kits and maps). The cordial, music-loving owners – bursting with tips and handy London knowledge – concoct an inclusive, homely atmosphere.

Rockwell   BOUTIQUE HOTEL **££**
(☏ 020-7244 2000; www.therockwell.com; 181-183 Cromwell Rd, SW5; s £120-125, d £145-180, ste from £200; ❋ @ 🛜; ⊖ Earl's Court) With an understated-cool design ethos and some lovely floor tiling, things are muted, dapper and more than a tad minimalist at the 'budget boutique' 40-room Rockwell. Spruce and stylish, all rooms have showers, the mezzanine suites are peaches and the three rooms looking on to the walled garden (LG1, 2 and 3) are particularly fine.

🛏 Notting Hill, Bayswater & Paddington

Don't be fooled by Julia Roberts' and Hugh Grant's shenanigans, Notting Hill and the areas immediately north of Hyde Park are as shabby as they are chic, but they're still cool.

Notting Hill & Bayswater

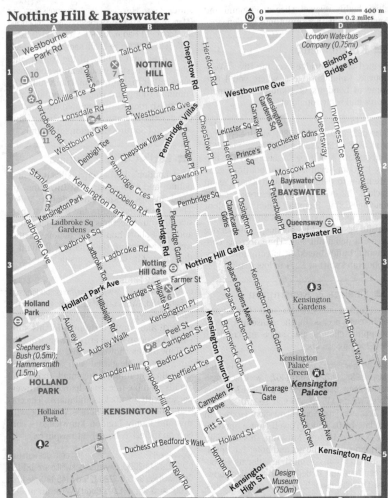

There are some gorgeous gated squares surrounded by Georgian town houses, but the area is better exemplified by the Portobello Road Market and the Notting Hill Carnival. Scruffy Paddington has lots of cheap hotels, with a major strip of unremarkable ones along Sussex Gardens that may be worth checking if you're short on options.

Safestay Holland Park HOSTEL £

(Map p122; ☑ 020-3326 8471; www.safestay.co.uk; Holland Walk, W8; dm £18, tw from £58, s from £66; ☎; ⊖ High St Kensington or Holland Park) This new place replaced the long-serving

YHA hostel running here since 1958. With a bright and bold colour design, the hostel has four- to eight-bunk dorm rooms, twin-bunk and single-bunk rooms, free wi-fi in the lobby and a fabulous location in the Jacobean east wing of Holland House in **Holland Park** (Map p122; Ilchester Pl; ⊙ 7.30am-dusk; ⊖ High St Kensington or Holland Park).

★ Main House HOTEL ££

(Map p122; ☑ 020-7221 9691; www.themainhouse. co.uk; 6 Colville Rd, W11; ste £120-150; ☎; ⊖ Ladbroke Grove, Notting Hill Gate or Westbourne Park) The four adorable suites at this peach of

Notting Hill & Bayswater

◎ **Top Sights**

◎ **Sights**

▣ **Sleeping**

✕ **Eating**

◎ **Drinking & Nightlife**

✪ **Entertainment**

◎ **Shopping**

a Victorian midterrace house on Colville Rd make this a superb choice. Bright and spacious, with vast bathrooms, rooms are excellent value and include endless tea and coffee. Cream of the crop is the uppermost suite, occupying the entire top floor. There's no sign, but look for the huge letters 'SIX'. Minimum three-night stay.

▣ Bloomsbury & St Pancras

One step from the West End and crammed with Georgian town-house conversions, these are more affordable neighbourhoods. A stretch of lower-priced hotels runs along Gower St and on the pretty Cartwright Gardens crescent. While hardly a salubrious location, St Pancras is handy with some excellent budget options.

★ **Clink78**   HOSTEL £
(Map p106; ☑020-7183 9400; www.clinkhostels. com/london/clink78; 78 King's Cross Rd, WC1; dm/r from £16/65 incl breakfast; @ �🛜; ⊖King's Cross/St Pancras) This fantastic 630-bed hostel is housed in a 19th-century magistrates' courthouse where Dickens once worked as a scribe and members of the Clash stood trial in 1978. Rooms feature pod beds (including overhead storage space) in four- to 16-bed dormitories. There's a top kitchen with a huge dining area and the busy Clash bar in the basement.

Parts of the hostel, including six cells converted to bedrooms and a pair of wood-panelled court rooms used as a cinema and internet room, are heritage-listed. There are all-female dorms too. You'll find an ATM and change machine conveniently in the lobby. Free breakfast included: toast and spreads, cereal, juice, tea and coffee (7am to 10.30am).

Generator   HOSTEL £
(Map p106; ☑020-7388 7666; www.generator hostels.com/london; 37 Tavistock Pl, WC1; dm/r from £18/68; @ �🛜; ⊖Russell Sq) With its industrial lines and funky decor, the huge Generator (more than 870 beds) is one of central London's grooviest budget spots. The bar, complete with pool tables, stays open until 2am and there are frequent themed parties. Dorm rooms have between six and 12 beds; backing it up are twins, triples and quad rooms.

London St Pancras YHA   HOSTEL £
(Map p106; ☑020-7388 9998; www.yha.org.uk; 79-81 Euston Rd, NW1; dm/r from £16/60; @ �🛜; ⊖King's Cross/St Pancras) This hostel with 186 beds spread over eight floors has modern, clean dorms sleeping four to six (nearly all with private facilities) and some private rooms. There's a good bar and cafe, although there are no self-catering facilities. Check out time is 10am.

Arosfa Hotel   B&B ££
(Map p106; ☑020-7636 2115; www.arosfalondon. com; 83 Gower St, WC1; incl breakfast s/tw/tr/f from £82/135/145/178, d £139-175; �🛜; ⊖Goodge St) The Philippe Starck furniture and modern look in the lounge is more lavish than the decor in the hotel's 16 rooms, with cabin-like bathrooms in many of them. About half have been refurbished; they are small but remain good value. There are a couple of family rooms; room 4 looks on to a small but charming garden. Prices rise on Saturdays.

Rough Luxe   BOUTIQUE HOTEL £££
(Map p106; ☑020-7837 5338; www.rough luxe.co.uk; 1 Birkenhead St, WC1; r £209-239; ✳⛜; ⊖King's Cross/St Pancras) Half-rough, half-luxury is the strapline of this nine-room hotel, and the distressed interior is true to its word. Scraps of old newspaper adorn the walls, along with original artwork, while the vintage 1970s TVs are for show only. Some rooms are admittedly small but service, location and the delightful patio garden at the back more than make up for it.

St Pancras Renaissance London Hotel

LUXURY HOTEL £££

(Map p106; ☑020-7841 3540; www.stpancras-renaissance.co.uk; Euston Rd, NW1; d from £230; ❋☞❋; ❸King's Cross/St Pancras) Housed in the former Midland Grand Hotel (1873), a Gothic, red-brick Victorian marvel designed by Sir George Gilbert Scott, the St Pancras Renaissance counts 245 rooms but only 38 of them are are in the original building; the rest are in an extension at the back and rather bland.

Clerkenwell & Farringdon

★Zetter Hotel & Townhouse

BOUTIQUE HOTEL £££

(Map p106; ☑020-7324 4444; www.thezetter.com; 86-88 Clerkenwell Rd, EC1; d from £222, studio £300-438; ❋❋☞; ❸Farringdon) ✎ The Zetter comprises two quite different properties. The original Zetter Hotel is a temple of cool with an overlay of kitsch on Clerkenwell's main thoroughfare. Built using sustainable materials on the site of a derelict office, its 59 rooms are small but perfectly formed. The Zetter Townhouse (Map p106; 49-50 St John's Sq; r £222-294, ste £438-480), on a pretty square behind, has just 13 rooms in a lovely Georgian pile.

At the main Zetter, the rooftop studios are the real treat, with terraces commanding superb views across the city. The rooms in the Zetter Townhouse are uniquely decorated in period style but with witty touches such as headboards made from reclaimed fairground carousels. The fantastic cocktail bar is a destination in itself.

Rookery

HERITAGE HOTEL £££

(Map p106; ☑020-7336 0931; www.rookery hotel.com; 12 Peter's Lane, Cowcross St, EC1; s/d £222/294, ste £474-660; ❋☞; ❸Farringdon) This charming warren of 33 rooms has been built in a row of 18th-century Georgian houses and fitted out with period furniture (including a museum-piece collection of Victorian baths, showers and toilets), original wood panelling shipped over from Ireland and artwork selected personally by the owner. Highlights: the small courtyard garden and the two-storey Rook's Nest penthouse suite.

East End & Docklands

★Qbic

DESIGN HOTEL ££

(☑020-3021 3300; www.london.qbichotels.com; 42 Adler St, E1; d £70-250; ❋☞; ❸Aldgate East) The 171 rooms of this snappy hotel south of Brick Lane are based around a 'cubi', with each bed and bathroom part of a square-box design. There's a very modern feel throughout, with white tiling, neon signs, and vibrant art and textiles. Rooms are sound-insulated, mattresses excellent and rainforest showers powerful. A great continental buffet breakfast is available for £9.95.

40 Winks

BOUTIQUE HOTEL ££

(☑020-7790 0259; www.40winks.org; 109 Mile End Rd, E1; s/d £120/195 incl breakfast; ☞; ❸Stepney Green) Short on space but not on style, this two-room boutique guesthouse, housed in an early-18th-century town house in Stepney Green, oozes quirky charm. Owned by a successful designer, the hotel has been used as a location for a number of fashion shoots and the rooms (the single is quite compact) are uniquely decorated with an expert's eye. Book far ahead.

✖ Eating

Dining out in London has become so fashionable that you can hardly open a menu without banging into some celebrity chef or other. The range and quality of eating options has increased exponentially over the last few decades. Waves of immigrant flavours have deeply infused London cuisine and the expectations of modern-day Londoners are demanding. In this section we have sieved out choicer restaurants and cafes noted for their location, value for money, unique character, ambience and, of course, good food. Vegetarians needn't fret: London has a host of dedicated meat-free joints, while most others have veggie offerings.

✖ West End

Mayfair, Soho and Covent Garden are the gastronomic heart of London, with a blinding choice of restaurants and cuisines at budgets to suit booze hounds, theatregoers or determined grazers.

★Shoryu

NOODLES £

(Map p78; www.shoryuramen.com; 9 Regent St, SW1; mains £9-15; ⏱11.15am-midnight Mon-Sat, to 10.30pm Sun; ❸Piccadilly Circus) Compact, well-mannered noodle-parlour Shoryu draws in reams of noodle diners to feast at its wooden counters and small tables. It's busy, friendly and efficient, with helpful and informative staff. Fantastic *tonkotsu* pork-broth ramen is the name of the game here, sprinkled with *nori* (dried, pressed sea-